# Gene Wilder
## FUNNY AND SAD

# Gene Wilder
## FUNNY AND SAD

BRIAN SCOTT MEDNICK

Published in the USA by:
BearManor Media
PO Box 1129
Duncan, Oklahoma 73534-1129
www.bearmanormedia.com

Printed in the United States of America.

Front Cover Image: © 1998 Metro-Goldwyn-Mayer Inc.
Back Cover Images: *(upper right)* © 1976 Twentieth Century-Fox Film Corporation; *(upper left)* © 1982 Columbia Pictures Industries, Inc.; *(left)* © 1974 Warner Bros. Inc.; *(bottom)* © 1974 Twentieth Century-Fox Film Corporation.

ISBN 978-1-59393-621-1

*For my mother, Bella Mednick,*
*who took me to his movies*

# Table of Contents

# Introduction

Seeing *Young Frankenstein* in a theater remains one of my earliest moviegoing memories. I couldn't have been more than five or six years old — and surely I couldn't have understood a lot of the adult humor — yet I remember loving it. When I was eleven, my local newspaper asked kids to write in about their favorite celebrity. While other kids my age wrote about Madonna, Cyndi Lauper, and Ralph Macchio, I wrote about Gene Wilder. Needless to say, I was a strange kid. When my fifth grade teacher once remarked that I looked like him, it was a bigger compliment than being told I looked like Tom Cruise, who had just emerged as the hottest young actor at the time. As I said, strange kid.

So why Gene Wilder? What is it about this neurotic Jewish guy from Milwaukee with a shock of frizzy blond hair that hooked me at such an early age? Well, I think it was probably a sense of identification. There are few lonely moviegoers out there who don't have at least one actor or actress they feel speaks directly to them. In every character Gene Wilder played, I saw a little bit of me. There is a very fine line between comedy and tragedy, and I can think of no other actor who walks that tightrope better than Gene Wilder.

As a childhood hero, Gene Wilder never let me down, and when I actually got to meet him briefly in 1993, he was just as charming, soft-spoken, and nice as I imagined he would be. As a biographer, I have tried my best to be as objective as possible about my subject. Gene Wilder is an intensely private person, and though he refused to cooperate with this book, he did write me a letter on December 15, 1996 in which he said, "I'm grateful you are not one of those people out to do some kind of exploitation hatchet-job." It would be hard to do a "hatchet-job" on Gene Wilder, for he is that rarity among celebrities — a gifted artist who is a genuinely decent person, something that comes across in his work.

I attempted to send Gene Wilder an early copy of my manuscript in the summer of 2000, but his manager informed me that he had no interest in seeing it. I understand where he is coming from and respect his privacy. I have a running joke when people ask me if Gene Wilder is a nice person. I say, "Yes…unless you're his biographer."

Like all of us, Gene Wilder has had his share of heartache, and like all of us, he is far from being perfect. His flaws do not make him any less of a person nor do they take away from his talent — if anything, they make him all the more human, a quality we often forget even the biggest stars possess. My goal was to document both his private and public life as tastefully and honestly as possible without turning this book into the very kind of sensationalistic celebrity bio he expressed gratitude to me for not writing.

Brian Scott Mednick
August 2010

"There's a lot to be said for making people laugh. Did you know that's all some people have?"

— *Joel McCrea as John Lloyd Sullivan*
*in* Sullivan's Travels *(1941)*

"My name was Jerry Silberman. I couldn't see 'Jerry Silberman in *Hamlet*.' Now, ironically, I can't see 'Gene Wilder in *Hamlet*' either."

— *Gene Wilder*

# 1

# Wisconsin: Where the Cheese Comes From

Jerome Silberman was twenty-seven years old and an aspiring young actor in January 1961. He had managed to get accepted into the prestigious Actors Studio, the champion of the Method style of acting taught by Lee Strasberg and practiced by Marlon Brando, Paul Newman, and Shelley Winters, to name a few. But there was one problem — his name. Jerry Silberman. It was an okay name for a nice Jewish boy from Milwaukee, but at a time when people with names like Bernard Schwartz were becoming Tony Curtis, it didn't seem like the appropriate moniker for someone intent on being a movie star. "If I start out as Jerry Silberman, it's going to be that for the rest of my career," he thought. "It'll be hard to switch it."

The night before he was to be introduced at the Actors Studio, Jerry's friend, writer David Zelag Goodman, came over, as did Jerry's sister Corinne and her husband Gilbert Pearlman, and they spent the entire evening trying to come up with a good stage name for Jerry.

"They started tossing out names," Jerry recalled. "And David rattled off about a thousand names, starting with A and working his way up. And none of them made emotional sense to me till he got to Wilder, and the bell went off. And I think it was because of Thornton Wilder, who wrote *Our Town*, which was one of my favorite plays."

The next day, the newly named Mr. Wilder decided to get rid of Jerry in favor of a name he was always quite fond of. "I had always liked Gene because of Thomas Wolfe's character Eugene Gant in *Look Homeward, Angel* and *Of Time and the River*," he said. He also had a distant relative, a navigator who flew thirty-three missions over Germany in World War II, and his name was Gene. Some time later his analyst would ask him, "Did you ever stop to think that your mother's name was Jeanne?" His answer was no.

And so Gene Wilder was born. "I thought it had a good sound," he said. Jerome Silberman had been born some twenty-seven years earlier, on June 11, 1933 at Mount Sinai Hospital in Milwaukee, Wisconsin, the second child and only son of William J. Silberman and Jeanne Baer.

William Silberman was a Russian Jew who emigrated to America with his family at the age of ten to escape the upsurge in anti-Semitism that was prevalent in Russia (his given name was Velvel, which was changed to William to make him sound more American). Born in Steppin, Russia on May 8, 1900 to Chaim Silberman and Tzeitel Waldman (they changed their names to Henry and Sarah upon coming to America), he arrived in Baltimore on March 31, 1911 with his parents and four siblings aboard a vessel called the *Chemnitz,* which had made its departure from Bremen, Germany. The family settled in Milwaukee at a house on 934 Walnut Street, and in 1916 Henry Silberman officially became an American citizen. He founded the H. Silberman Novelty Company in 1917, which became the Continental Distributing Company in 1929. In addition, he was president of a realty firm, as well as president of his local Hebrew congregation.

William attended North Division High School in Milwaukee. He hated school and often cut class to go to the lakeside and watch boats or spend time at the public library. Though he wasn't a good student, William loved to read and was the first in the family to become fluent in English. A knee injury prevented him from playing football, so he took one semester of needlepoint, which he enjoyed and got so good at it that it became his main hobby into adulthood, something which embarrassed Corinne when she was a teenager, but not Jerry (Gene still has needlepoint pillows that his father made).

William took over his father's business and renamed it Bill's Specialty Company. He specialized in importing souvenirs and chocolates from Holland, which he then sold to discount stores. He later moved on to manufacturing such items as miniature beer and whiskey bottles and gag glasses that gave the illusion they were filled with real drinks when they weren't.

Jeanne Silberman was a Polish Jew whose family hailed from Warsaw. She was born in Chicago on August 29, 1907 and had studied to be a concert pianist. She came to Milwaukee in 1928 and shortly thereafter married William. Gene contrasted his mother and father's personalities by describing William as "very innocent, very naive," and calling Jeanne "very artistic, temperamental, very loving, but oh, so volatile."

They moved into a house at 1052 53rd Street and on May 14, 1929 welcomed their first child into the world, Corinne Ruth. The couple later moved to 3172 North 44th Street, which is where Jerry spent the early part of his youth before the family moved for the last time to 3732 North 54th Boulevard.

Jeanne was active in local Jewish organizations, such as Hadassah and the Milwaukee Home for Aged Jews, but she was plagued with health problems — a heart attack she suffered when her son was eight years old left her a semi-invalid.

"The doctor — Samuel Rosenthal was his name — big, heavyset fellow who sweated a lot, and he said two things that changed my life," Gene recalled. "The first one was, 'Don't get angry or it might kill your mother.' I almost didn't recover from that one. I only got over it when I was about thirty-three years old."

The second thing the doctor told him was to make her laugh if he could. So, to cheer his mother up, little Jerry would improvise skits, do accents, and act out Danny Kaye routines. It was at this young age that the boy who would become world famous for his hyper on-screen antics learned that being funny got him attention. He succeeded in making his mother laugh and recalled, "I knew I scored when she peed in her pants…I was nine years old…I don't know what I said that could be so funny, but when I saw I was on a roll, I kept on going and just made up things. And then she said, 'Oh, Jerry! Oh, Jerry!' and she'd run off to the bathroom."

When Jerry was eleven, his mother suffered her second heart attack and went to Florida to recuperate. One night Mrs. Silberman said to the residents of the hotel they were staying at, "Now Jerry will entertain you." The young boy got nervous and didn't know what to do. At this point he didn't consider himself an entertainer and had no routines. So he looked at the crowd and said, "I'll now give my imitation of a little boy going to bed." And he proceeded to walk out, close the door, and go to bed. "I suppose I tried for a laugh even then," he later confessed.

For a brief and terribly unhappy time, Jerry's parents sent him off to the now torn down Black-Foxe Military Institute in Hollywood, California where, as the only Jewish boy in the school, he was constantly the victim of abuse by his fellow students, most of whom were products of broken homes. "It was not pleasant," Gene told Dick Cavett in 1991. "My mother was ill and I think she thought that I would learn to play bridge and dance and play the piano and grow up and become Tyrone Power in *Diplomatic Courier*."

"I couldn't bring myself to write home about the things that began happening," Gene told Merv Griffin. "The kids would beat me up, insult me, put shoe polish on my pubic hairs, some stunt like that, every day I was there. Actually, it wasn't terrifying because I didn't understand what anti-Semitism was, and I didn't know why the boys were doing these things. I kept asking myself 'Why?' All I could figure out was that I looked a little roly-poly and pudgy. I didn't know what anyone could have against me personally."

Jerry was bitten by the acting bug after seeing Corinne in a dramatic recital of Guy de Maupassant's "The Necklace" at the Wisconsin Conservatory of Music. He was so envious of the attention she received from the audience that after the recital he approached her acting teacher, Herman Gottlieb, and told him that he wanted to study with him. Gottlieb told the eleven-year-old boy that if he came back in two years and was still interested he'd take him on. The day after his thirteenth birthday, Jerry went to Gottlieb and studied with him for five years.

His debut came in 1948 when he played Balthasar in *Romeo and Juliet* at the Milwaukee Playhouse. In the beginning, Jerry was intent on pursuing comedy. "I wanted to be whatever Danny Kaye was," he said. "That's what I wanted to be. Then I wanted to be what Jerry Lewis* was. Then I wanted to be what Sid Caesar was."

At sixteen, Jerry traveled to Poughkeepsie, New York to perform in summer stock at the Reginald Goode Summer Theater. On his way there, he stopped in New York City where he saw the original Broadway production of Arthur Miller's *Death of a Salesman* with Lee J. Cobb. It was something of a life-changing experience and geared him towards pursuing serious drama, which he deemed more important. "I didn't know acting like that existed," Gene said. "I saw a great, *serious* performance — not in a movie, but in a live performance right in front of me. And I thought to myself: 'There's a big difference between what *he's* doing and what *I'm* doing.' It was then that I realized I was a 'bedroom actor.'"

Gene describes a "bedroom actor" as someone who basically maps out his entire performance the night before while standing in front of a mirror, carefully working out every physical gesture and movement. "I even got to the point where I'd make little notes on syllables of words to say whether I should go up or down in pitch," he said. "Then I read *An Actor Prepares* by Stanislavsky and everything that had been brewing inside me since seeing Cobb's performance suddenly made sense. Not how to do it, but what I was aiming for."

When he returned from summer stock, Jerry cast himself as Willy Loman and, along with two friends, began doing his own three-character version of the play, which he performed for schools and women's clubs in Milwaukee.

Despite his ability to express himself onstage, Jerry was a very shy kid whose "heart would pound if I had to speak in public," he said. "I was aggressive from a distance but not really aggressive at all. I had a great inability to express hostility. I was the kind of kid

---

* In a 2002 phone conversation the author had with Jerry Lewis unrelated to this book, Lewis said he had "such high regard" for Gene Wilder and regretted that they never met. Lewis also said he understood Gilda Radner was a fan of his.

in high school who would be in love with the girl who thought I was a schnook. A girl in another class would think I was her dream. But I wouldn't care about her. And all the time I'm saying to myself, if only I could act with the first girl the way I act with the girl I don't care about…"

As a chubby kid who was shy around girls, abused in military school, and constantly seeking love and approval from his parents, performing was a sanctuary for Jerry in that it allowed him to escape whatever demons haunted him at the time by taking on the role of someone else.

"I was sexually embarrassed as a youth, but I had gigantic visions…" Gene once said. "I can't tell you of my crazy sexual fantasies. I used to be so ill at ease meeting girls that at an early age I turned to acting to make better use of my frustrations involving the opposite sex." Gene's shyness with women carried over into early adulthood, for he did not lose his virginity until he was twenty-four years old, late even by 1950s standards.

In a 1986 interview with *Entertainment Tonight*'s Barbara Howar, Gene Wilder spoke about performers like himself who learned early on that entertaining people seemed the only way to feel accepted. "Something went wrong when they were two or three or four or five years old," he said. "There was a crack in the psyche someplace and they had to slip on a banana peel or sing a song or do a tap dance in order to get the love and affection and recognition that made them feel loved. And that carries on later on in life. All of us are looking for [applause]. And that lasts for about two days. And then, like heroin, you would need it again. And it's a terrible sickness."

After graduating Washington High School in Milwaukee in 1951, Jerry attended the University of Iowa, where Corinne had gone as well. He majored in theater and was active in student pro- ductions of plays. While there, he joined Alpha Epsilon Pi, the premier Jewish fraternity in North America, of which he remains a lifelong brother. During vacations, he played in summer stock, and in 1955 obtained his Bachelor of Arts degree.

Wanting a classical training in the theater, in 1955 Jerry enrolled in the Bristol Old Vic Theatre School in Bristol, England, where he studied fencing, gymnastics, judo, and voice. When he reached the courses that concentrated on acting techniques, he left because "they were teaching all sorts of silly nonsense about drawing room comedies and how to laugh and things, and I didn't want any part of that." His fencing instruction ended up proving worthwhile, though, since it enabled him to earn money as a fencing instructor on his return to the States. He would also later choreograph the fencing scenes for Shakespeare's *Macbeth* and *Twelfth Night* at the Cambridge Drama Festival in Massachusetts.

Upon his return from England, Jerry was drafted into the army and assigned to the Valley Forge Hospital in Phoenixville, Pennsylvania. He optioned to work in the neuropsychiatric ward where he was confronted by paranoid schizophrenics who, amongst other things, believed they were gorillas and Jesus Christ. "I should have been a patient," he said, "but I wasn't. I was what they call a neuropsychiatric specialist, and I got into an awful lot of trouble." As an actor, Gene feels that his experience there helped to enrich his later performances. "The one thing it did for me was allow me to play people who were just barely in touch with reality or, let's say, who were slightly in touch with another reality."

It was during this time that Jerry's mother passed away, succumbing to congestive heart failure on November 18, 1957 at the age of fifty (she had been diagnosed with breast cancer the year before but was too weak to receive treatment). She never got to see her son become a success or even know him by his new name. "[My dad and I] were walking down the street together," Corinne recalled many years later, "and the marquee said 'Gene Wilder,' and my dad was so moved, and, of course, his first reaction was, 'Too bad momma wasn't here to see this.'"

Following Jeanne's death, William began developing a close relationship with Belle Hurwitz (nee Fromstein), a widow four years his junior, with whom he and Jeanne had been friends for years. Eighteen months after Jeanne's death, they married on May 26, 1959. Jerry and Corinne were glad that their father had found a companion and took well to the marriage, which lasted fourteen years until William's death from cancer on May 30, 1973 at age seventy-three.

Even after William's death, Gene kept in contact with Belle, sending her flowers on her birthday and talking on the phone with her. Corinne would come to Milwaukee every summer and visit with her. Belle died in 1986 at the age of eighty-two, leaving behind four children from her first marriage — Burton, Earl, June, and Lawrence — with whom Gene and Corinne, despite no ill will, never kept in contact.

Most of Jerry's fellow army inductees wanted Saturday and Sunday as their days off, but Jerry requested Monday and Tuesday so he could travel to New York to attend acting classes at the HB Studio. Among his classmates were Sandy Dennis, Dustin Hoffman, and Charles Grodin, whom Jerry befriended and would later work with professionally. While Grodin thought Jerry was a good actor, he didn't think he'd ever be able to make it in the business because he didn't have the traditional pretty boy actor look of the 1950s. In his autobiography, Grodin recalled, "There was this funny-looking boy in class named Jerry Silberman, and everyone thought: My God, what is a guy who looks like that going to do in this profession?!"

As irony would have it, Gene Wilder found stardom a number of years before Charles Grodin, despite his "funny looks."

"My friends all told me that my wife was too good for me and after a couple of years I decided they were right."

— *Gene Wilder*
*as George Caldwell in* Silver Streak *(1976)*

# 2

# A Career in Bloom

Gene Wilder is a private person and has no qualms about letting anyone, particularly interviewers, know it. "I don't mind talking personal," he says, "because it's the only thing I want to talk about. But I don't like to talk about private. And I won't talk about private." One may naturally ponder what the difference between personal and private is. To find out, all you have to do is ask him a question. If the question is personal, he'll be happy to answer it. If it's private, that's another story.

Gene doesn't look to get publicity for himself and tends to shy away from Hollywood parties and movie premieres. He's even antsy about doing publicity for his own movies. "When it comes time to sell a film," he said, "I don't like to sell because that would make me nervous. But I have an obligation, after a year and a half's work, to wave a little red flag a week or two weeks before the film comes out, and say, 'The circus is coming! The circus is coming! Hello, everybody!' And then when the circus is playing and everyone knows it's there, go home and forget about it till the next time."

While he grants television and print interviews when he has a new film coming out, Gene has largely avoided appearing on the major late night talk shows because they have studio audiences that expect guests to be funny, and Gene doesn't think he's a particularly funny person offscreen. "Put me on *The Tonight Show* or some big show with an audience and I would be very nervous," he told Bob Costas in 1989 on his show *Later*, which Gene felt comfortable doing since Costas didn't have an audience. "I don't mean I couldn't do it, but I'd say it's not worth it."

Despite the above quote, Gene actually was a guest on *The Tonight Show*, but only once, on June 12, 1970 to promote *Quackser Fortune Has a Cousin in the Bronx*. David Steinberg was guest host. Though Gene was still in the early stages of his film career, Steinberg recalled, "Gene was already in the stratosphere of comic geniuses...a totally original, unique comic entity." Gene never appeared on David Letterman's NBC or CBS programs, and it would be thirty-five years after his *Tonight Show* appearance before he would go on another comedy talk show when he visited *Late Night with Conan O'Brien* to plug his autobiography in 2005. "I hope I didn't do anything to traumatize him," Steinberg joked.

Gene apparently feels more comfortable doing daytime talk shows. In 1978 he and Dom DeLuise were guests on Phil Donahue's program to promote *The World's Greatest Lover*. In 1979 Gene appeared on both Merv Griffin and Dinah Shore's talk shows, but requested tapings without a studio audience or other guests. "To be on with all those other guests, and to know you have to deliver dynamite lines...I don't like being funny on shows like that," he said. "In movies, I'm funny. On TV, I'd like to let people know what I'm really like." Gene has been a guest on various talk shows in Europe over the years and more recently has appeared on *The View* and *The Martha Stewart Show* (on the latter, after Gene discussed his book *My French Whore*, Stewart showed him several ways to cook asparagus).

Since he is so private, Gene Wilder never spoke at length about his first two marriages until writing about them in his 2005 memoir. Both marriages ended in divorce and produced no children. Gene married Mary Mercier, an actress and playwright, on July 22, 1960. They appeared together in Gene's first New York play, Arnold Wesker's *Roots*, in 1961 at the off-Broadway Mayfair Theatre.

Mary was born in Cardiff, Wales. She spent her early childhood in Wales and London before moving to Los Angeles as a teenager.

Unhappy with the lack of theater work in L.A., she moved to New York to pursue acting. In 1967 she wrote a Broadway play called *Johnny No-Trump*, which was a major disaster, closing after five previews and just one opening night performance. Mary stopped writing plays and in the 1970s moved back permanently to Los Angeles where she worked as executive secretary at the Actors Studio West. She had a few small film roles, appearing as one of the passengers in *Airplane!* (1980) and as waitresses in *Mistress*, a 1992 comedy that Robert DeNiro co-produced and co-starred in, and Diane Keaton's *Unstrung Heroes* (1995).

Mary is very reluctant to talk about her marriage to Gene, which ended in 1965. When asked to give an interview for this book, she declined, saying the whole subject "dredged up some painful, difficult memories...It's difficult to talk about."

Gene married Mary Jo Ayers, a former college roommate of Corinne's who was several years his senior, on October 27, 1967. Gene had actually met Mary Jo — or "Jo," as her close friends called her — years earlier at a party when he was seventeen and drove down to visit Corinne at the University of Iowa. He found Jo strikingly beautiful but thought she was out of his league because he was an awkward teenager and she was an older college girl. Despite spending most of their time at the party together and even sharing a long kiss, the two would not see each other for another fifteen years, when Corinne would again introduce them.

The couple made their home on the Upper East Side of Manhattan at 110 East 70th Street. Jo had a daughter from a previous marriage named Katie, born on June 4, 1960, whom Gene adopted shortly after marrying Jo. For years, Gene refused to publicly discuss his first two marriages and would only say of Jo, "She's a very nice lady."

According to friends, the pressure of Gene's career and being away from home so much contributed to the breakup. Gene also fell in love with another woman while married to Jo, having what he himself described to *Newsday*'s Leo Seligsohn in 1977 as a "traumatic" affair in Paris in 1968. "I fell in love in Paris," Gene told Seligsohn. "It was a hopeless situation because I had to leave and did leave after four months." Thirty years later, speaking of the Paris affair, he told *Scotland on Sunday*'s Catherine Deveney, "I thought I was in love. We never even made love."

It was Gene's choice to end the marriage, and by the time their divorce became final in 1974, Jo had only hurtful feelings towards Gene. This all had a devastating effect on Katie, who never knew her real father and went into therapy as a result of the divorce. Sadly, Gene has been estranged from Katie since the mid-1980s.*

Gene and Jo managed to keep their marital woes private to most of those who knew them. When Bud Yorkin, who directed Gene in *Start the Revolution Without Me*, heard of Gene's split from Jo, he was quite surprised. "I thought they got along quite well," Yorkin said. "I saw him a lot socially after the picture. I saw him in New York. And I remember he told me in his quiet manner and I was really stunned. I saw no evidence of any [trouble]."

Before his stage career bloomed in the early 1960s, Gene paid the bills — just barely — by working as a chauffeur and selling toys at FAO Schwarz. Gene's wife Mary and friends such as Charles Grodin were doing similar things to get by. "When we weren't working, we all walked around and lived on our unemployment checks and ate chuck steak," Gene recalled. "I got $35 a week in unemployment and my rent was $100 a month, so I soon ran out of money. I just couldn't manage. I used to allot myself $7.50 a week for incidentals, which meant clothing and doctors and entertainment and car fare and everything else you spend money on to live."

In 1961 Mary had been cast in the off-Broadway play *Roots*. Gene asked her if she could get him an audition. She did, and director Mark Rydell, who would go on to direct such films as *The Rose* (1979) and *On Golden Pond* (1981), cast Gene as Mary's husband. One night, Rydell's agent, Lily Veidt, widow of German actor Conrad Veidt, came to see the play and afterward asked Gene if he had representation. He told her no. "She started representing

---

* Katie was always a very emotionally unstable person. While Gene was occupied caring for Gilda in Los Angeles, Katie was hospitalized in New York with a severe case of endometriosis that required surgery. She was upset that Gene did not lavish the same attention on her that he did on Gilda. Gene made numerous attempts to contact Katie, but she refused to respond to him, and the two have not had any contact in twenty-five years.

me," Gene said, "and I got a Television Play of the Week: Maxwell Anderson's *Wingless Victory*. Irene Mayer Selznick [who produced *A Streetcar Named Desire* on Broadway] saw *Victory* and asked me to try out for *The Complaisant Lover*, which was about to be done on Broadway starring Michael Redgrave. I tried out and got the part."

Graham Greene's *The Complaisant Lover* marked Gene's Broadway debut in November 1961, and as the bewildered Dutch hotel valet, Gene received the Clarence Derwent Award for the best performance of the 1961-1962 season in a non-starring role. Gene went on to tour with *The Complaisant Lover* and then appeared in the road production of *The Millionairess* with Carol Channing before returning to Broadway in 1963 in Bertolt Brecht's *Mother Courage and Her Children*.

Landing the role of the chaplain in *Mother Courage* was perhaps the luckiest break of Gene's career, not because of his success in the play, which closed after only fifty-two performances, but because its star was Anne Bancroft. Bancroft was dating Mel Brooks, whom she would later marry and who often hung around backstage after the play. Brooks, already well-known then for the *2000 Year Old Man* LP's he did with Carl Reiner, told Gene that he was writing a screenplay and there was a part that Gene would be perfect for.

"He had written thirty pages of a screenplay called *Springtime for Hitler*," Gene recalled, "and he read it to his girlfriend Anne Bancroft and me one Saturday evening out at Fire Island. And he said, 'Do you want to play this part? As I go on writing it, I'll write it for you.'" Gene said yes to Brooks' offer, but it would be years before he would hear from him, so during most of the 1960s, Gene occupied himself with a lot of Broadway and television roles.

He was in the original 1963 Broadway production of Ken Kesey's novel *One Flew Over the Cuckoo's Nest* with Kirk Douglas. In it he played Billy Bibbit, the stuttering young sanitarium patient later played by Brad Dourif in the 1975 film. Douglas had loved Kesey's novel so much that he bought the stage and film rights to it. When he heard that Dale Wasserman also was interested in acquiring the rights to *Cuckoo's Nest*, Douglas asked him to do the adaptation and gave Wasserman the stage rights while keeping the film rights for himself. Douglas tried out the play in New Haven and Boston before heading to Broadway, where it opened on November 14, 1963 at the Cort Theatre.

Despite rave reviews out of town, *Cuckoo's Nest* failed miserably in New York and closed after two months. Eight days after its opening on Broadway, President Kennedy was assassinated. Gene and his fellow actors went on as scheduled that night, but, according to Douglas, "There was a numbness in the people on the stage and in the audience."

Gene got the role in *Cuckoo's Nest* through the intervention of Charles Grodin. Grodin had been asked to play Billy Bibbit himself, but he didn't feel he was right for it. He suggested to director Alex Segal that he audition Gene. Segal had never heard of Gene, but upon Grodin's recommendation met with him and cast him. Gene found it to be a rather unpleasant working relationship. "I can't stand screamers, especially when they take it out on the poor actor who can't answer back," Gene said of Segal. "If someone can't yell at Kirk Douglas, they'll yell at some pipsqueak, in this case, it happened to be me. I don't like that…I didn't think he was a good director." Although *One Flew Over the Cuckoo's Nest* was not a hit, Gene remained unscathed and received a New York Drama Critics Circle Award nomination for Best Supporting Actor.

Gene would later return the favor to Grodin when his friends Joseph Bologna and Renee Taylor would ask him to direct their play *Lovers and Other Strangers*. "There's a man named Charles Grodin in Los Angeles," Gene told the couple. "Take your work to him, and he will know what to do." Bologna and Taylor took his advice, and after meeting with Grodin, decided Gene's instincts were right. Grodin directed the play and went on the road with it before it hit Broadway, where it ran for seventy performances.

After *Cuckoo's Nest* closed on January 25, 1964, Gene went on to appear on Broadway in *The White House* with Helen Hayes and the musical *Dynamite Tonight*, both in 1964, and was Alan Arkin's understudy in Murray Schisgal's *Luv*, which opened in November of that year. After Arkin left the role of Harry Berlin, Gabriel Dell took over, followed by Gene, who stayed with the three-character play until it closed on January 7, 1967.

On television, Gene appeared in several of NBC's *The DuPont Show of the Week* presentations, playing Wilson in "The Interrogator," a reporter in "Windfall," and Muller in "A Sound of Hunting" with Peter Falk and Sal Mineo, all in 1962. That same year he had the role of headwaiter on an episode of *The Defenders* entitled "Reunion with Death" and also played the role of Yussel in the *Armstrong Circle Theatre* broadcast of "The Man Who Refused to Die" on CBS. In 1966 he appeared as Yankel in "Home for Passover" on NBC's *The Eternal Light*. And in a nice twist of fate, the boy who was entranced by Lee J. Cobb's performance in *Death of a Salesman* on Broadway got to play opposite Cobb, albeit in a small role, in the Emmy-winning 1966 production of Arthur Miller's play on CBS. It reunited Gene with director Alex Segal, whom, despite their confrontational offstage relationship during *Cuckoo's Nest*, Gene now considered a friend. The cast included Mildred Dunnock as Linda, James Farentino as Biff, and George Segal as Happy. Gene had the role of the uptight Bernard.

While it would seem like Gene Wilder's entrance into the movies would be precipitated by Mel Brooks, it was actually Warren Beatty and director Arthur Penn who were responsible for giving Gene his first film role. They had seen him on Broadway and asked him to play the part of Eugene Grizzard, the meek undertaker that the notorious Barrow gang takes for a ride in *Bonnie and Clyde*.

When we first see Eugene, he's sitting on the porch, kissing his best girl Velma (Evans Evans), when he spots the Barrow gang stealing his car. "I had to start out my first day of my first picture — first five minutes — kissing this girl, who was Evans Evans," Gene recalled. "And Arthur Penn said, 'I'd like to introduce you. This is Evans Evans, Gene Wilder. Do you want to just get into it a little bit and then we'll start?' And we started kissing and then he said, 'Action!' And then afterwards we said, 'How are you? It's nice to meet you.'"

Since he only had seven minutes of screen time and was acting with the undeniably gifted likes of Beatty, Faye Dunaway, Gene Hackman, Michael J. Pollard, and Estelle Parsons, all of whom received Oscar nominations, Gene more or less went unnoticed, despite the film's enormous success. Still, he made the most of his appearance, adding a huge dose of humor to a film that was otherwise grim and downbeat. In playing Eugene Grizzard, Gene displayed hints of the kind of idiosyncratic behavior that would later become his hallmark — his meek demeanor, his tendency to suddenly burst into fits of hysteria, his infectious, wheezy laugh. And it's understandable that Gene may have felt some sort of connection with his first film role, since, aside from the fact that they shared different forms of the same first name, they also shared the same home state. When Bonnie asks Eugene where he's from, he replies, "I'm from Wisconsin originally...where the cheese comes from."

Upon its initial 1967 release, *Bonnie and Clyde* drew criticism from many for its supposed glorification of murder, as well as its graphic violence. The film is now considered a breakthrough for its time, having ushered in the "New Hollywood" era of American filmmaking. It received ten Academy Award nominations, including Best Picture, and won Oscars for Estelle Parsons' supporting performance as Hackman's wife Blanche and Burnett Guffey's cinematography that so hauntingly captured the look of the Depression-era Southwest. But it was not the kind of role destined to make Gene a star. For that he would have to wait until the following year when Mel Brooks would finally make good on his promise.

"I didn't hear from him for three years," Gene said. "I thought he'd forgotten me, but it took him that long to raise the money to do it." While Gene was appearing in *Luv*, Brooks and producer Sidney Glazier visited him backstage. Brooks already had Zero Mostel committed to do the film and told Gene, "The only thing is, Gene, Zero doesn't know you at all. I'm sorry to put you through this, but you're going to have to do a reading for him."

Gene assumed he had the part wrapped up. After all, Brooks specifically wrote it for him and the thought of having to audition never entered his mind. "My heart was pounding as I walked to Sidney Glazier's office," Gene said. "I went up the elevator and my heart was pounding harder. I knock at the door. There's Mel and Sidney and Zero. Zero gets up and walks towards me and I'm thinking, 'Oh, God, why do I have to go through this again? I hate auditions, I *hate* them.' Zero reached out his hand as if to shake hands and then put it around my waist and pulled me up to him and kissed me on the lips. He gave me a big kiss on the lips. And all my fear dissolved. We sat down and read a scene from the script."

A half hour after Gene left his meeting with Mostel, Brooks called him and told him that Mostel liked him. The role was his.

*Springtime for Hitler* was retitled *The Producers* because, according to Gene, "Joseph E. Levine [who financed half the budget] said, 'You can't say *Springtime for Hitler* — the Jews in the Midwest won't accept that.'" Brooks had originally begun writing it as a novel, but it was too talky, so he turned it into a play. But Brooks found his play had too many locations, so he ultimately turned it into a screenplay (it would take Brooks more than three decades to realize that maybe a stage version of *The Producers* wasn't such a bad idea after all).

Filmed in eight weeks on a budget of $946,000, *The Producers* tells the story of Max Bialystock (Mostel), a once-great theatrical producer now reduced to scamming money off of little old ladies. One day, a hapless young accountant named Leo Bloom* (Wilder) walks in on Max in his office to find him cavorting with one of his admiring grannies. Shocked, Bloom stutters and stammers before Max tells him to "just say oops and get out."

Leo waits outside until Max bids his lady farewell. He then informs Max that he was sent to do his books. Max invites him in and preaches about his lost fortunes. "I'm wearing a cardboard belt!" Max tells him.

"It was right out of my own life experience," Brooks said of *The Producers*. "I once worked with a man who did make serious love to very old ladies late at night on an old leather office couch. They would give him blank checks, and he would produce phony plays. I can't mention his name because he would go to jail. Just for the old ladies alone he would go to jail."

As Leo goes over Max's books, he finds that Max committed a small case of fraud, but, after begging and pleading, Max convinces Leo to "move a few numbers around" so he can avoid jail. It is then

---

* Mel Brooks is too well-read for the name Leo Bloom not to have intentionally been borrowed from James Joyce's protagonist Leopold Bloom in *Ulysses*. Ironically, Zero Mostel played the character of Leopold Bloom off-Broadway in 1958 and later on Broadway in 1974 in *Ulysses in Nighttown*, a play based on Joyce's novel.

that Leo comes to the realization that a producer could actually make more money with a play that's a flop than a hit if, certain that the show would bomb, he raises more money than he actually needs to produce the show. If the show closes immediately, the investors wouldn't have to be paid back and the producer keeps the leftover cash.

This starts the wheels turning in Max's head as he convinces Leo to become his partner as they go in search of the worst play ever written. After searching through piles of scripts, and even rejecting Kafka's *Metamorphosis* because it sounds too good, they find a play they feel is destined to flop: *Springtime for Hitler*, "a gay romp with Adolf and Eva in Berchtesgarten," written by a crazed *Fuehrer*-worshipping Nazi named Franz Liebkind, played by Kenneth Mars. Brooks originally cast a then unknown Dustin Hoffman as Liebkind. Hoffman got a call to fly to L.A. to do a screen test for director Mike Nichols for the leading role in *The Graduate*. Brooks, thinking Hoffman had no chance of being cast opposite his wife Anne Bancroft, let Hoffman go. After Hoffman got the part, Brooks himself considered playing Liebkind, but after holding auditions, he was so impressed with Mars that he gave the role to him.

After convincing Franz to let them do the play, Max and Leo hire a hilarious array of characters: a then svelte Christopher Hewett as Roger De Bris, the pretentious director who seems more at home in an evening gown than a theater; Dick Shawn as LSD, who stumbles into the wrong audition, only to be cast as Max and Leo's hippie Hitler; and Lee Meredith as Ulla, the sexy Swedish secretary Max hires to work in his lavish new office, even though she can barely speak a word of English.

On opening night, Max and Leo watch as the audience looks on in shock at their opening production number in which Nazi storm troopers sing the praises of *der Fuehrer*. Brilliantly choreographed by Alan Johnson and featuring Brooks' hysterical lyrics ("Don't be stupid, be a smarty/Come and join the Nazi party!"), the *Springtime for Hitler* number joins "the bean scene" from *Blazing Saddles* as the most famous scenes from any of Brooks' films.

After audience members begin leaving the theater stupefied, Max and Leo repair to the bar down the street and celebrate what they

are certain will be the biggest flop ever to hit Broadway. But at inter-
mission, as droves of theatergoers rush in for a drink, they overhear
conversations in which *Springtime for Hitler* is being lauded as the
funniest show in years. They go to the theater to see for themselves
and find the entire house in stitches at LSD's unique interpretation
of Adolf Hitler. Alas, Max and Leo's plan backfires, leading Max to
woefully analyze the situation: "I was so careful. I picked the wrong
play, the wrong director, the wrong cast…Where did I go right?"

Though early test screenings proved negative and at one point the
film was going to be shelved, sneak previews in New York started a
word-of-mouth campaign that ultimately resulted in lines around
the block. The picture slowly opened up in other cities and eventually became a moneymaker.

Despite varying reports that Brooks and Mostel's personalities
often clashed during the making of *The Producers*, Gene claims
not to have noticed any friction and found the entire experience
extremely rewarding. A lot of that had to do with how Zero Mostel
took the young actor under his wing. "You may have heard stories
about how bombastic, aggressive, and dictatorial Zero might be,"
Gene said. "It didn't happen with me. He always took care of me. I
loved him. He looked after me as if I were a baby sparrow."

Gene would often have dinner with Mostel and was fascinated
about the days when he was blacklisted. "It wasn't a consuming
passion for him then," Gene recalled. "It was a scar, but it had
healed, and he was on to a very productive career and was happy in
his life as far as I could tell." Gene said when it came to those who
named names before the House Un-American Activities Com-
mittee, Mostel "mellowed, but he didn't forgive. He may have had
compassion for the people who informed because they were weak,
but he didn't forgive."

At the time of release, *The Producers* received mixed reviews, but
it is now an undisputed classic that Roger Ebert has called "the
single funniest movie I've seen since I've been a film critic." Some
critics in 1968 had different opinions. "Thoroughly inept and vile"
was how Andrew Sarris characterized it, while Pauline Kael found it
"amateurishly crude" and Arthur Schlesinger Jr. called it "an almost
flawless triumph of bad taste, unredeemed by wit or by style."

Critics aside, *The Producers* had one supporter in Peter Sellers, who had seen an advance screening of the movie and called it "the ultimate film" and "the essence of all great comedy combined in a single motion picture." Sellers took out ads in two West Coast newspapers lauding the film, and while not all critics at the time shared Sellers' enthusiasm, luckily for Brooks enough members of the Academy of Motion Picture Arts and Sciences did — they awarded him the Oscar for Best Story and Screenplay Written Directly for the Screen. Gene did not go unnoticed either — he received a nomination for Best Supporting Actor. His competition was Seymour Cassel in *Faces*, Daniel Massey in *Star!*, Jack Wild in *Oliver!*, and Jack Albertson, who took home the award for *The Subject Was Roses*. "I was just praying that I wouldn't get the award because I'd have to get up and make a speech, and I was too nervous to make the speech," he half-joked. "I wanted to win if they had said I was in England doing something and accepting on behalf of Gene Wilder, here is Mel Brooks or something."

*The Producers* also received Golden Globe nominations for Best Screenplay and for Mostel's performance, but, unlike the Oscars, Gene was overlooked in the Best Supporting Actor category.

*The Producers* was a breakthrough film for both Gene Wilder and Mel Brooks. Already known for being a master funnyman, Brooks now showed he could be a first-rate film director. And now Gene was able to show off his talents in a role that was tailor-made for him in a medium that reached a much larger number of people than your average Broadway audience. Leo Bloom was a star-making role, not unlike what Benjamin Braddock was for Dustin Hoffman in *The Graduate* a year earlier. Brooks maintains that *The Producers* "would have been a very good comedy with Zero Mostel and another comic...But Gene Wilder made it a classic."

After *The Producers*, Gene Wilder was well on his way to becoming one of the major stars of the approaching '70s.

# 3

# You Say You Want a Revolution

Following his success in *The Producers*, Gene Wilder chose his next film projects wisely. After receiving his Oscar nomination, *The Hollywood Reporter*'s Hank Grant wrote that Gene was in "dueling competition with Dustin Hoffman for the title role in *Portnoy's Complaint*." Alas, Richard Benjamin got the role of Alexander Portnoy, a lucky break for both Wilder and Hoffman, considering how poorly received the film version of Philip Roth's novel of Jewish angst was.

It was important now for Gene to show that he was more than just a good stage actor who got lucky with one great film role, and the 1970 comedy *Start the Revolution Without Me* allowed him to do this. The film was produced and directed by Bud Yorkin, who, along with executive producer Norman Lear, brought *All in the Family* to television the following year.

Co-starring with Gene was Donald Sutherland, who, with the release of *MASH* that same year, was himself just emerging as a major star. Gene was cast before Sutherland, though, and when Yorkin and Lear were searching for someone to play the role of Gene's brother, Gene suggested Charles Grodin. But Grodin, who was a relative unknown at the time and could have used a part like this, was too committed to *Lovers and Other Strangers* to consider doing the movie. Besides, Yorkin wanted to have a contrast between the two brothers and felt that Wilder and Grodin had too many similar qualities.

*Start the Revolution Without Me* is pure unadulterated silliness, the kind of material Gene Wilder is most at home with. Orson Welles narrates the film, which is set during the French Revolution and tells the story of two sets of mismatched twins (both played by Wilder and Sutherland) — one peasants, the other aristocrats — who are switched at birth and wind up meeting during a revolutionary battle. Hugh Griffith plays the scatterbrained King Louis XVI, who is so utterly clueless that his wife (Billie Whitelaw) romances her lovers in their bed as Louis sleeps.

Filmed entirely on location in France with a mostly French crew, the film went into production as *Two Times Two*, but Warner Bros. executives hated the title and insisted it be changed. The film had a budget of just under $2.5 million. Gene was paid $60,000, while Sutherland received $45,000, a far cry from the multimillion-dollar salaries they would receive later on in their careers. Making the film was a thoroughly satisfying experience for Gene, who had Jo and Katie with him during the seven-week shoot. An avid Francophile, Gene took delight in discovering small out-of-the-way restaurants and new French wines.

The filming of *Start the Revolution Without Me* required several fencing scenes and allowed Gene the opportunity to demonstrate his adroitness with a sword. "Everybody was stunned when he got into these sword fights and all of a sudden Gene became an animal!" Yorkin recalled. "Here we had stuntmen that were going to try to teach him how to hold up a sword and protect himself. Before long, all the stuntmen were protecting themselves."

The film opened in New York on February 4, 1970 to many positive reviews, but it failed to become a big moneymaker, something Yorkin blames on bad blood between himself and a studio executive. "It didn't make a lot of money," Yorkin recalled, "because the gentleman who was head of distribution for Warner Bros. at that time, who I had a very tough relationship with, didn't like the picture, so it never got an opportunity, despite all the reviews that it got. I have a book full of pretty terrific reviews, and yet Warner

Bros. released it with not a lot of prints. So it never had the success that I thought it deserved."

Pauline Kael was not among the critics whose kind words took up room in Bud Yorkin's scrapbook. She called Yorkin's direction "flaccid," noted that "the script doesn't hold up," and dismissed Sutherland, who she said "smirks and mugs his way through his dual role." On a more positive note, she wrote, "The picture turns silly, but at least it doesn't turn sour. It's worth mentioning mainly for Hugh Griffith, who is oddly poignant as a befuddled Louis XVI, and for Wilder. Wilder has a fantastic shtick. He builds up a hysterical rage about nothing at all, upon an imaginary provocation, and it's terribly funny. It's the sort of thing one wouldn't expect to work more than once, but it works each time and you begin to wait for it and hope for it — it's a parody of all the obscene bad temper in the world. Wilder's self-generated neurasthenic rage could become a lasting part of our culture, like Edgar Kennedy's slow burn."

Despite Ms. Kael's dismissal and its lackluster performance at the box office, *Start the Revolution Without Me* joins Carl Reiner's *Where's Poppa?* (1970) and Hal Ashby's *Harold and Maude* (1972), both starring Ruth Gordon, as one of a handful of offbeat films from the early '70s that are now considered cult classics. "What's really interesting," Yorkin said in 1996, "is when I go to a university or something to talk, particularly in the last ten years, invariably I always expect most of the questions [to be like], How'd you get *All in the Family* on the air? But I'm amazed at the cult following that this picture has. I mean, when I went up to Harvard and spoke at the *Lampoon*, the only thing they wanted to talk about — and I think they ran that night — was *Start the Revolution*."

According to Yorkin, people still approach him till this day quoting lines from the movie, such as Richard Dreyfuss, who once came up to him and said, "I thought it was a costume ball," citing the scene in which Griffith's King Louis shows up at a formal affair dressed in a bird suit.

# 4

# The Luck of the Irish

Gene turned down an offer to star in Mike Nichols' film version of Joseph Heller's novel *Catch-22* to instead do Waris Hussein's *Quackser Fortune Has a Cousin in the Bronx*, a quirky little film released in the summer of 1970 that today remains one of Gene's lesser known efforts, even though it garnered him some of the best reviews of his career. It was also a good vehicle for him in that it showed he could carry a picture all by himself, which is the mark of any great leading man. In his two films prior to this, Gene shared equal time with other highly skilled actors. But *Quackser* is definitely his show.

In the film, Gene plays the title character, a poor Irish schlep who makes his living following around the horses of Dublin and collecting their manure, then selling it for fertilizer. He's viewed as something of an oddity by his family, who can't understand why he doesn't just get a job at the local foundry where his father and the rest of the neighborhood men work.

One day, a car speeds by and accidentally runs Quackser and his cart off the road. After getting his cart repaired, the girl in that car spots Quackser and begins chatting with him. She's Zazel (Margot Kidder), an American coed going to Trinity. Though they come from two very different worlds, they begin to develop a romance that is beautifully played out in Gabriel Walsh's screenplay.

Since Gene needed to affect an Irish accent, he spent a month in Dublin trying to pick up the speech patterns of the locals. "I just roamed around and heard an awful lot of dialects — all different," he said. "After a while you'd learn to spot them — that was North of the Liffey, that was South of the Liffey [the river that runs through Dublin]. I heard a lot that I knew I'd never be able to use, because no one would understand a word I said. I finally combined the pronunciation that I heard from the guide we hired to drive us around and the lilt I heard in a woman who owned a restaurant where we sometimes ate."

*Quackser Fortune Has a Cousin in the Bronx* was the first film to show the romantic side of Gene Wilder, an aspect that very few of his later characters lacked. His Quackser is not your typical dashing movie hero. He's poor, simple, and basically a slob. Yet Gene brings such humanity to the part that we can't help but see why Zazel falls for him.

The critics also fell for him. Judith Crist found the film "a pleasant piece of fluffery that does little but showcase further the charming talents of Gene Wilder." Other reviewers were even more impressed. *Time* magazine called it "one of the most delightful comedy dramas in recent years." "Gene Wilder's performance is sad, exuberant, open and touching," said Gene Shalit. "Everyone ought to have a lovely time as this earthy, romantic comedy." Penelope Gilliatt wrote in *The New Yorker*, "Gene Wilder, one of the best American actors, plays the dreadful Quackser as best as man could." And Rex Reed called it "one of the year's major surprises" and wrote, "Elliott Gould and Dustin Hoffman can move over because Gene Wilder, as Quackser, is a funny-tragic new kind of anti-hero who is more than just another pretty face...he's dynamite!"

# 5

# Chocolate and Sex

In Roald Dahl's popular children's book *Charlie and the Chocolate Factory*, the character of Willy Wonka is described as follows: "Covering his chin, there was a small neat pointed black beard — a goatee. And his eyes — his eyes were most marvelously bright. They seemed to be sparkling and twinkling at you all the time. The whole face, in fact, was alight with fun and laughter."

Sans the goatee, Dahl could have very well been talking about Gene Wilder, who would go on to play Mr. Wonka in the film version of Dahl's 1964 book. The film was going to go into production as *Charlie and the Chocolate Factory*, but, presaging the political correctness of today, some in Hollywood at the time felt that the word Charlie was an anti-black putdown, even though when Dahl wrote the book the thought of Charlie being a slur of any kind never crossed anybody's mind. So, due to this most inane of protests, the film was retitled *Willy Wonka & the Chocolate Factory*. The 1971 musical gave Gene the chance to display his ample singing talents and give one of his most eccentric and memorable performances.

The film was directed by Mel Stuart, whose background was mainly in documentaries, but who had directed two features prior to this, *If It's Tuesday, This Must Be Belgium* (1969) and *I Love My... Wife* (1970). The idea for a film of *Charlie and the Chocolate Factory* came about when Stuart's young daughter approached him and said he should make a movie out of this book she had read. Stuart, who was vice president of David Wolper Productions, read the book, thought it had great potential, and brought it to David L. Wolper. Wolper wanted to do the film entirely in animation, but Stuart thought it could work as a live-action feature. So Wolper, well-known in Hollywood for his deftness at swiftly putting projects together, got Quaker Oats to put up the film's three million dollar budget. Quaker Oats also planned to manufacture a Wonka chocolate bar upon the film's release, but, despite the fact it would have been a great marketing move, never got around to it.

Once the three million dollars was secured, Wolper had gotten Paramount Pictures to agree to distribute the movie, but during the course of filming Wolper left Paramount for Warner Bros., who ended up releasing the film.

Before casting the lead, Stuart and Wolper filled the roles of the children and their parents. Stuart was particularly taken with one actress who read for the part of Mrs. Teevee. "I said, 'This is fantastic,'" recalled Stuart. "'She is the most fabulous actress. I can't stand it! I got to have her! I got to have her!'" But the actress had a hard time deciding whether to do *Willy Wonka* or commit to doing a sitcom she was offered. Stuart desperately hoped she would agree to do his film, but ultimately she opted for the sitcom. The actress was Jean Stapleton and the sitcom was *All in the Family*.

Dodo Denney was cast in Stapleton's place, and once the rest of the kids and parents were cast, the obvious question Stuart and Wolper had was, Who's going to play Willy Wonka? Stuart and Wolper held their casting session in New York's Plaza Hotel. Joel Grey came in and auditioned. They liked him, they knew he could sing, and physically he was suited to the part since in Dahl's book Wonka is described as a diminutive man. The next actor to come in was Gene.

As soon as he looked at him, Stuart turned to Wolper and said, "Dave, this is Willy Wonka! This is fantastic! There can't be anybody else."

"Shhh!" Wolper shot back. "Don't tell him! Don't tell him! If he knows it'll cost us more money."

After Gene finished his reading and was about to leave, Stuart just couldn't restrain himself. He ran after him as he was about to get on the elevator and told Gene, "You've got it. I don't care. We'll make a deal. You got the part."

After winning the role of Wonka, Gene came up with an idea for how he should make his entrance in the film, and felt so strongly about it that he basically told Stuart he wouldn't do the film unless he could enter that way. "I would like to come out with a cane and be crippled," Gene recalled telling Stuart, "and walk along — everyone quiets down…until just before I get to the gate, my cane sticks into a cobblestone, stays there, I look at it, realize I don't have my cane, and start to fall forward and do a forward somersault, jump up on my feet and everyone applauds…because if I do that, no one will know from that time on whether I'm lying or telling the truth, [and] I do lie throughout that picture." Stuart gave into Gene's request and later called it a "brilliant idea."

With the title role now cast, Stuart then went on to fill some of the film's lesser parts, including hiring an array of dwarves and midgets, most of whom couldn't speak a word of English, to play the workers in Wonka's factory known as Oompa-Loompas, who more or less serve as the film's Greek chorus as they comment in song about the children's bad behavior.

Stuart was firm in insisting that none of the other parts be played by stars. Both Sammy Davis Jr. and Anthony Newley wanted to play the candy store proprietor, a role that would have allowed them to perform "The Candy Man" on-screen. But Stuart felt having a well-known personality in that role would detract from the reality of the film, so he instead cast an unknown British actor named Aubrey Woods to play the part. Davis still benefited, however, as his version of "The Candy Man" became an enormous hit, as well as one of his signature songs.

As was the case with his two previous films, *Willy Wonka* sent Gene abroad to work, this time to Munich, Germany. The film was like a lot of children's books in how it tried to convey a moral to its young readers. In telling of a poor, honorable boy who triumphs over a bunch of spoiled brats, the film condemned gluttony, vanity, and watching too much television.

Peter Ostrum, in his one and only film role (he's now a veterinarian in upstate New York), plays the film's hero, Charlie Bucket, a paperboy who supports his family, which consists of his single mother and two sets of grandparents, all four of whom share the same bed. When Willy Wonka, the world's greatest chocolate manufacturer, announces that he will give a tour of his secretive factory to five lucky children who find gold tickets in his Wonka bars, the children of the world tear through bar after bar in search of that precious golden ticket.

Charlie's closest confidant is his Grandpa Joe (Jack Albertson, who just a few years earlier beat out Gene for the Oscar), who hasn't gotten out of bed in twenty years. Grandpa Joe fills Charlie with hope and tells him that he will definitely find one of Wonka's golden tickets. After the fifth ticket is uncovered, however, Charlie is understandably down, but then it's revealed the fifth ticket's owner made his own fake, leaving one real ticket out there somewhere. And, just like in the movies, Charlie finds some money on the street, buys a Wonka bar, and, yes, discovers the fifth golden ticket.

Each winner is allowed to bring one guest to Wonka's factory, so Charlie asks Grandpa Joe to come with him. Even though he hasn't been out of bed in two decades, Grandpa Joe manages to put his feet to the floor and accompany his grandson on Wonka's magical tour.

The four other children on the tour are a parent's nightmare. There's Augustus Gloop, a poster boy for childhood obesity; Violet Beauregarde, whose excessive gum-chewing would put even Burt Reynolds to shame; Veruca Salt, the quintessential daddy's little rich girl; and Mike Teevee, couch potato extraordinaire.

As the tour progresses, each one of the children "disappears" due to their bratty behavior. In the end, the only one left is Charlie, who remains decent and honest, something Wonka admires so much that he decides to give Charlie his factory.

*Willy Wonka & the Chocolate Factory* is, in the strictest sense, a children's movie, yet its appeal is so much greater. Refreshingly, it is not sugary sweet. It treats the rotten kids in a darkly humorous way that most adults will savor. In fact, Stuart insisted that he wasn't making a children's movie at all. "I was making an adult picture and the little brats can come along and laugh," he said. "I have a tremendous respect for children...as far as their capacity to 'get it.'"

Though Roald Dahl is credited with adapting his book to the screen, his version of the script ended up being almost entirely rewritten by another writer. Few would deny Dahl's gifts as an author of children's fiction, but he wasn't a very skilled screen-writer. "He took the book too literally," Stuart said. "And things that would work in a book won't work in the reality of film...So I had a young kid secretly come to Munich with me and locked him in a room and said, 'I want you to rewrite the script.' And he rewrote the script. And a great deal of the script was really the work of this kid."

That "kid" was David Seltzer, who went on to write *The Omen* (1976) and later wrote and directed the films *Lucas* (1986) and *Punchline* (1988).

When word got out that Seltzer was rewriting his script, Dahl became furious. He insisted Stuart personally come to his home in London and show him the revamped script or he'd publicly lash out against the film and reveal it was being ghostwritten. Stuart flew from Munich to London and presented Dahl with the script. Dahl went up to his bedroom, slammed the door, and for the next two hours, as Stuart patiently waited downstairs, read the script. When he emerged from his room, he threw the script at Stuart and said, "Well, all right, I guess it's okay."

"He knew the kid had beaten him," Stuart later said.

Seltzer's talents also helped Stuart out in a pinch when, on the last day of shooting, Stuart realized that the ending line just didn't work. In Dahl's version, Charlie, Grandpa Joe, and Mr. Wonka are in the Wonkavator as it crashes through the factory roof and magi-cally floats in the sky. In Dahl's script, the closing line has Grandpa Joe uttering, "Yippee!"

"My God," Stuart said when he read it. "I can't end the picture with Grandpa saying yippee. That's terrible."

By this time, Seltzer was back in the U.S. "I don't care where he is," Stuart told one of his assistants. "Go find him on the phone. Everybody's standing by." Eventually Stuart found Seltzer, who was vacationing in a cabin in Maine in an attempt to recuperate from the whole Wonka experience. Stuart got on the phone and told Seltzer, "I got a set here. I got blue screen. I got Gene Wilder...I want an end line and I want it right away."

"All right," Seltzer replied. "How much time have I got?"

"Two minutes."

"Okay."

Sixty seconds later, Seltzer returned to the phone.

"Here's the last line," he said:

> WONKA
> *Charlie, don't forget what happened to the man*
> *who suddenly got everything he always wanted.*
> CHARLIE
> *What happened?*
> WONKA
> *He lived happily ever after.*

"Brilliant fairy tale ending line," Stuart said. "I knew the kid was great."

Dahl never showed up on the set during the entire forty-day shoot, and after the film's release badmouthed it in private circles, saying it was a total disaster.

To design the elaborate sets, Stuart hired Harper Goff, who created some truly dazzling effects, including a chocolate waterfall and a colorful array of gadgets and gizmos. Among the edible delights Goff created in Wonka's factory were large candy mushrooms, an innocent enough concoction that some young people in the early '70s read a little too much into. "Everybody thought when the people were eating the mushrooms it was a psychedelic trip that was coming up," Stuart recalled. "But I never meant it as a psychedelic trip. I just thought the mushrooms looked kind of interesting. All the kids from the '70s [said], 'Man, that was real cool!'"

All of the Wonka sets were torn down immediately after shooting wrapped to make way for the cast and crew of *Cabaret* (1972), which started filming in the same studio the day after *Willy Wonka* finished. Had Joel Grey, who played the Master of Ceremonies in

*Cabaret*, been cast as Wonka, he would have found himself getting to know Munich quite well.

To do the film's songs, Stuart hired Leslie Bricusse and Anthony Newley, whose score was Oscar-nominated, and whose memorable songs, aside from "The Candy Man," also include the lesser known though arguably superior "Pure Imagination." (In 2010 AT&T used Gene's performance of "Pure Imagination" in a television commercial.)

Stuart found working with Gene to be an incredibly positive experience. "It's no mystery," he said, "there are actors in Hollywood you don't want to direct because it's not worth your life. I can name a few, but I won't. But with Gene there was none of that…It was a very smooth set because everybody was excited by what was going on."

According to Gene, however, Stuart "was a maniac who screamed and yelled, not at me, but at the crew, not realizing that you can't yell at one person on the crew without having it affect every actor who's going to act in that scene."

Stuart was impressed with Gene's attention to detail in playing Wonka, such as how he deliberately made his hair appear frizzier and more out of control as the picture progressed. "He really thought that out and worked on that to slowly make the guy seem more demented as he was going along," Stuart said.

Gene also impressed everyone when he wasn't in character. The food in Munich wasn't particularly good, so Gene and his colleagues found themselves mainly eating trout when they dined out, as it was the most edible dish there. When Thanksgiving came, Gene paid for an elaborate turkey dinner for the entire cast and crew. And though he got along with his young co-stars, according to Stuart, he never really stopped being Willy Wonka during the five weeks they were in Munich. "I have found that the very good actors become their persona off the set," Stuart said, "so Gene was always slightly aloof."

Roger Ebert has said that *Willy Wonka & the Chocolate Factory* is "probably the best film of its sort since *The Wizard of Oz*. It is everything that family movies usually claim to be, but aren't: Delightful, funny, scary, exciting, and, most of all, a genuine work of imagination."

For his performance, Gene received a Golden Globe nomination for Best Actor in a Motion Picture — Musical or Comedy, but lost to Topol in *Fiddler on the Roof*.

Even though *Willy Wonka* is one of his best loved films, Gene was disappointed in it. "It was a film that could have been a great picture, but there would have had to be another director," Gene said. "At the time they were so worried about the NAACP and offending blacks so they changed the Oompa-Loompas into orange-faced, green-haired men that I guess were supposed to be something like the munchkins and that wasn't the point at all. It was the relationship that Willy Wonka had with the people from another country whom he'd saved. You know, they missed the whole point. It was about love. So they said, well let's not take a chance on offending anybody."

Despite *Willy Wonka*'s classic status, it actually didn't make a great deal of money when it opened. Thanks to home video, however, the film is more popular today than it was in 1971. More recently, ABC has taken to showing the film in prime time once a year. And, to mark the film's twenty-fifth anniversary, Warner Bros. re-released it nationally with a new print in the summer of 1996, a rare move that proves *Willy Wonka & the Chocolate Factory* will likely go on to be one of Gene Wilder's most enduring films, whether he likes it or not. "I don't want my gravestone to say: WILLY WONKA LIES HERE," he said in 2002.

In 2005 Warner Bros. remade *Charlie and the Chocolate Factory* with Tim Burton directing and Johnny Depp starring as Wonka (contrary to an early rumor that the role of Willy Wonka was going to be played by rocker Marilyn Manson). The film kept Dahl's original title and was a non-musical. Dahl's widow Liccy, who had full approval over the film, felt, as did her late husband, that the 1971 version didn't quite capture Dahl's book.

Prior to the film's release, Gene said the new adaptation was "all about money" and that there was no need to make a new movie adaptation of the book. "I like Johnny Depp, and I appreciate that he has said on the record that my shoes would be hard to fill," Gene said. "But I don't know how it will all turn out. Right now, the only thing that does take some of the edge off this for me is that Willy

Wonka's name isn't in the title." Gene later stated that, if the new adaptation "has to be done," Depp was a good choice to play Wonka, even though Gene refused to see the film.

*Everything You Always Wanted to Know About Sex But Were Afraid to Ask* was the title of Dr. David Reuben's best-selling book that gave Woody Allen inspiration for his bawdy, star-studded 1972 comedy. In his book, Dr. Reuben dealt with many questions and concerns relating to human sexuality, which Allen himself proceeded to answer in his own inimitable fashion. The film is divided into seven separate vignettes, each dealing with one of the topics Reuben covered. Among them: "Do aphrodisiacs work?" "Are transvestites homosexuals?" "Why do some women have trouble reaching an orgasm?"

The most popular segment of the movie, however, is titled "What Is Sodomy?," featuring Gene as a mild-mannered doctor who falls in love with a sheep. When Allen first approached Gene for the role, he didn't tell him what the script was about. Instead, he told him that he wanted to do his own version of Theodore Dreiser's novel *Sister Carrie* with either Gene or Laurence Olivier, who played the role opposite Jennifer Jones in the 1952 film version called *Carrie*. "But instead of Jennifer Jones, I want to use a sheep," Allen told Gene. After that, Gene was hooked.

As the sodomy segment opens, we see Gene as Doug Ross, a young physician with his own practice. He lives in a beautiful home and is happily married to his wife Anne (Elaine Giftos). But one day, a shepherd named Stavros Milos (Titos Vandis) comes to his office all the way from Armenia. When Dr. Ross asks him what his problem is, he replies, "I am in love with a sheep." After Milos tells the good doctor how his relationship with Daisy the sheep has deteriorated, a horrified Dr. Ross tells him he can't help and that he would be better off seeing a psychiatrist.

But Milos won't take no for an answer and brings Daisy into the office. From then, it's love at first sight as Dr. Ross agrees to see Daisy privately to try to help find out why she's been so distant to Milos. But he instead romances her, two-timing his wife by spending long afternoons with Daisy in a luxurious hotel suite and buying her expensive gifts. His wife slowly begins to suspect something, though. "Darling, is it my imagination or do you always smell from lamb chops?" she asks.

Eventually, Anne catches Daisy and her husband in bed together, and it's downhill for the doctor as he loses his wife, his money, and his medical license. He's denigrated to waiting tables in a Jewish delicatessen, but then his true loss comes when Milos takes Daisy back to Armenia, leaving the desperate doctor in the gutter guzzling Woolite.

*Everything You Always Wanted to Know About Sex But Were Afraid to Ask* was a hit, grossing $8.8 million and becoming the ninth biggest moneymaker of 1972. To this day, Doug Ross remains one of Gene's very favorite roles. He was also quite fond of his wooly co-star. "I did like that sheep," he said. "The one that you saw in the movie had a little black ring around both its eyes and it made it very…I guess you could say sexy…But the standby — you have to have more than one sheep — if that sheep gets sick all the filming would stop. So, the sheep that had the sexy eyes was a boy. And the standby was a girl. But the girl wasn't very attractive. So I worked with this boy. And it was very interesting, except when the boy got nervous and we were in bed, 'cause the bed was a mess afterwards."

The film gave Gene the opportunity to work with yet another great comedian who, like Mel Brooks, successfully made the transition to filmmaker. "Woody is one of the nicest people I have ever met," Gene said. Having worked with both Brooks and Allen, Gene talked about their very different styles in a 1978 interview with Kenneth Tynan in *The New Yorker*. "Working with Woody is what it must be like to work with Ingmar Bergman," Gene said. "It's all very hushed. You and I are talking quietly now, but if we were on Woody's set someone would already have told us to keep our voices down. He said three things to me while we were shooting — 'You know where to get tea and coffee?' and 'You know where to get lunch?' and 'Shall I see you tomorrow?' Oh, and there was one other thing — 'If you don't like any of these lines, change them.' Mel would never say that. The way Woody makes a movie, it's as if he were lighting ten thousand safety matches to illuminate a city. Each of them is a little epiphany, topical, ethnic, or political. What

Mel wants is to set off atom bombs of laughter. Woody will take a bow and arrow or a hunting rifle and aim it at small, precise targets. Mel grabs a shotgun, loads it with fifty pellets, and points it in the general direction of one enormous target. Out of fifty, he'll score at least six or seven huge bull's-eyes, and those are what people always remember about his films."

# 6

# A Very Good Year

1974 was a very good year for Gene Wilder, professionally anyway. While his personal life saw his six-year marriage to Jo come to an end, his movie career was in full swing. Four films with his name in the credits were released theatrically and his first TV movie aired.

The TV project was *Thursday's Game*, a comedy-drama Gene did in 1971 that was intended as a theatrical feature but laid in limbo for several years before being aired as a telefilm on ABC. *Thursday's Game* was directed by Robert Moore, who would go on to direct the Neil Simon movies *Murder by Death* (1976) and *Chapter Two* (1979). James L. Brooks, creator of *The Mary Tyler Moore Show* and *Taxi*, wrote and produced the film.

In *Thursday's Game* Gene plays Harry Evers, the producer of a daytime game show called *Let's Chance It*. Every Thursday, Harry and his buddies meet up for a night away from the wives and a good old-fashioned game of poker. After a fight breaks out between some of the guys, the Thursday night games stop, but Harry and his friend Marvin (Bob Newhart) feel they still need one night of the week to themselves. So the two don't tell their wives the game has broken up and continue meeting on Thursdays, trying to find something to do as Harry's marriage to Ellen Burstyn and his career both start falling apart.

The supporting cast reads like a who's who of some of the '70s' best-known sitcom stars. In addition to Newhart, the cast includes Nancy Walker as Mrs. Bender, the sympathetic job counselor who plays amateur psychiatrist to Harry; Cloris Leachman as Marvin's neurotic, older wife whom he contemplates leaving; Valerie Harper as a co-worker Harry almost has an affair with; Rob Reiner as Harry's airhead agent, who doesn't even realize Harry is his client; and Norman Fell as Harry's boss, whose office Harry proceeds to wreck after he tells him he's fired.

As for Gene Wilder's theatrical films in 1974, two of them remain among his most successful and acclaimed works, while the other two are barely remembered. *Rhinoceros*, the film version of Eugene Ionesco's 1960 play about the dangers of conformity, reunited Gene with Zero Mostel. It was a production of the American Film Theatre, whose intent was to film renowned plays and show them only twice in an attempt to make the films a rare event, not unlike live theater (years later, however, the films went into general distribution). Gene plays Stanley (Berenger in the play), an alcoholic clerk who remains human as everyone around him, including his best friend John (Mostel), transforms into the titular pachyderm.

*Rhinoceros* was directed by Tom O'Horgan, who had directed *Hair*, *Jesus Christ Superstar*, and *Lenny* for the stage. According to Gene, O'Horgan's approach to directing was "not to do or say much, because he believed it would all evolve by itself…[That] might work for a musical like *Hair*, but it doesn't work in a movie. It was chaos, and you've got to have planning in a movie." Gene thought the situation might have been helped had a producer been present on the set to keep O'Horgan in line, but Gene said "there was never a producer there."

Gene admitted that he "did not really understand the play at first, but I wanted to work again with Zero." Despite the re-teaming of Wilder and Mostel, the material did not approach the comic heights of *The Producers* and the film was rejected by critics and audiences alike. Vincent Canby of *The New York Times* made note of the film's "clumsy, badly choreographed slapstick" but praised what he deemed "an extremely attractive performance by Gene Wilder." Even Ionesco himself had problems with O'Horgan's treatment of his play. "It was a bad film," he said, "and it destroyed the meaning of my play."

Not quite as disastrous was Stanley Donen's musical film version of Antoine de Saint-Exupéry's children's book *The Little Prince*. Filmed at Elstree Studios in Herts, England, the film starred Richard Kiley as an aviator who makes an emergency landing in the Sahara Desert. There he befriends a golden-haired young boy (Steven Warner) from another planet and teaches him about life as he learns of the boy's strange encounters traveling through the universe.

Gene was one of several actors in small roles who meet up with the little prince during the course of the film. With long frizzed-out hair and a brown suit, Gene played the part of a fox the little prince tames. As in his other children's musical, *Willy Wonka & the Chocolate Factory*, *The Little Prince* again allowed Gene to sing, this time in an exhilarating Lerner and Loewe number about learning to trust.

"One of the best things I've ever done in a film was in a bad picture, which was *The Little Prince*," Gene said. "But I was good as the Fox. I worked hard. I loved the book and I loved my part, and I loved the six weeks that I worked alone in the woods with a little boy and a director and a small camera crew and playback machine. Then I saw the rest of the picture and I didn't know what my sequence had to do with the rest of it. They didn't understand the book, and yet the director cried when he talked about it so it wasn't a lack of feeling for it, but it was just misconceived."

Gene Wilder's biggest hits of 1974 were courtesy of Mel Brooks. *Blazing Saddles*, released in February, and *Young Frankenstein*, released in December, were huge commercial and critical hits that, along with *The Producers*, are today considered the best work of both Wilder and Brooks.

Brooks, whose career has been based on poking fun at established movie genres, found the perfect target in the Hollywood western. *Blazing Saddles* is inspired lunacy, a movie that, like Brooks, will do anything for a laugh. The film was the brainchild of Andrew Bergman, who drew his inspiration from a poster he had seen of Jimi Hendrix in a cowboy outfit on a horse. His original draft was titled *Tex-X*. Brooks loved the script and brought in Norman

Steinberg to collaborate on it. Steinberg in turn brought Alan Uger and Richard Pryor onboard to contribute to the script as well. Uger clashed with Brooks and was gone in a week. Pryor, whose drug problems made him notoriously unreliable, was gone in two weeks. Before ultimately being called *Blazing Saddles*, the title was changed to *Black Bart*, and, despite all five writers' names appearing in the credits, the bulk of the script was actually written by Brooks, Bergman, and Steinberg.

Set in the backward little town of Rock Ridge, the film tells what happens when greedy land barons send a black man named Bart (Cleavon Little) to be the new sheriff. Of course, he doesn't stand a chance of being accepted — let alone surviving — in this bigoted town, but that's just the point. Their plan is to ransack Rock Ridge, driving the residents out so they can build a railroad through the town.

Bart is immediately rejected by the citizens of Rock Ridge. His only friend is an alcoholic former gunslinger named Jim, who years earlier was known as the Waco Kid, the fastest gun in the West. Brooks' first choice to play the Waco Kid was Johnny Carson. One night after appearing on *The Tonight Show*, Brooks offered Carson the role but he turned it down, insisting he was not an actor (as his only two film appearances — in *Looking for Love* (1964) and *Cancel My Reservation* (1972) — proved).

"You would be great as this character, though," Brooks told him. "You would be just like Dean Martin in *Rio Bravo*." Carson still wouldn't do it, so Brooks offered Dan Dailey the role, but he couldn't accept it due to health problems. Brooks next approached Gig Young after seeing him in *They Shoot Horses, Don't They?* (1969). The part may have been a bit too close to home for Young, for he really was a chronic alcoholic, and when he showed up on his first day to film, Young started foaming at the mouth and literally fell on his face due to alcohol withdrawal (four years later, Young killed his wife before taking his own life).

Brooks was now in a bind and called Gene in New York, asking him to do the role as a favor. Brooks had originally offered Gene the role that Harvey Korman plays in the finished film, but Gene turned him down (he actually wanted to play the Waco Kid from the very beginning). Brooks needed Gene to start filming right away, and though Gene wanted to help Brooks out, he was scheduled to fly to London the next day to begin filming *The Little Prince*. Gene called Stanley Donen and informed him of the situation, so Donen accommodated Gene by moving his scenes to the end of the shooting schedule. The next day, Gene was in Los Angeles getting outfitted for the role and getting acquainted with the horse he would ride in the film. "He saved my life," Brooks said. "He's not only a genius actor but he's a good friend. And he never said, 'I told you so.'"

When Bart first encounters the Waco Kid, he is hanging upside down in a jail cell. Bart asks him, "What's your name?" He responds, "Well, my name is Jim, but most people call me…Jim."

"Gene did not look in my mind like the Waco Kid," Brooks said. "I thought he was too young, too Jewish. Gene taught me a great lesson — typecasting stinks. Just go for a good actor."

In addition to Gene, many soon-to-be Brooks regulars were on hand, including Korman as the greedy Hedley Lamarr; Madeline Kahn as Lili von Shtupp, a dance hall girl fashioned after Marlene Dietrich; Dom DeLuise, who camps it up in small role towards the film's end; and Brooks himself in dual roles as a Jewish Indian chief and the crooked governor who does impressions of Harpo Marx.

Little's role was originally intended for Richard Pryor. Brooks and his fellow writers thought Pryor would be great in the lead, but his known problems with drugs and his unreliability didn't make studio executives keen on casting him. In his 1995 autobiography, Pryor made no mention of drugs being the reason he didn't get the role. "I knew *Blazing Saddles* was going to be one of the funniest scripts ever," Pryor wrote, "and before we even finished writing it Mel was talking about me starring as the black sheriff. But when it came time to make the movie I think people at the studio more powerful than Mel didn't want me.

"They were scared of my reputation. Yes, I was funny, nobody could deny that. But they also saw me as a volatile, vulgar, profane black man who wisecracked about getting high and screwing white women. It scared the shit out of their Brooks Brothers sensibilities to think about risking millions of dollars on a movie starring a person like me.

"I think Mel liked me," Pryor continued, "and I think he could've fought to keep me as his star. I think Cleavon Little did a good job. However, I know what kind of job I could've done. But Mel, bless his heart, had a decision to make, and he chose to get his movie made."

Though *Blazing Saddles* sends up the western, Brooks also has fun tearing apart the structure of movies in general. As the film heads towards its conclusion, everything gets so chaotic that all of the characters wind up busting through the soundstage of the Burbank Studios where food fights occur in the commissary, a movie musical turns into a brawl, and Bart and Jim ultimately decide to just go to a movie (the movie they see, by the way, is *Blazing Saddles*).

When discussing Mel Brooks, the issue of taste invariably arises. Brooks has never been known for his tact, and after showing the completed film to Warner Bros. executives, was ordered to edit out several scenes, such as when Lili, the morning after having slept with Bart, very suggestively offers him an obscenely phallic German sausage for breakfast. And then there's the movie's most talked about moment, known in polite circles as "the bean scene," in which a bunch of cowboys are sitting around the campfire having a dinner of baked beans and get an attack of flatulence. Brooks, ever the savvy businessman, made sure his contract gave him final cut, so despite the protests from Warner Bros., those moments remain in the film.

Brooks' scatological humor didn't please everyone. *Washington Post* critic Gary Arnold wrote, "Brooks is so preoccupied with the idea of acting outrageous that he neglects to give the material any style or unity...Brooks writes naughty punch lines in the same way little kids try out naughty expressions on their parents, and what makes you wince is not the expressions themselves but the ignorant, indiscriminate way they're being used." Of Gene's role, Arnold wrote, "Wilder's benign detachment is rather endearing in the crude, overbearing context of this film; it's as if Brooks didn't have the heart to subject him to the indignities he had in store for the other clowns. Nevertheless, one wonders what *Blazing Saddles* might have been like if Richard Pryor and Gene Wilder had been paired in full-bodied comic roles and Brooks had given the material some pertinence and control."

Pauline Kael also panned the film, observing that Brooks "doesn't have the controlling vision that a director needs. It's easy to imagine him on the set, doubled up laughing at the performances and not paying any attention to what he's supposed to be there for." Kael once again praised Gene, though. "Gene Wilder saves himself by performing in his own dreamer's rhythm, giving his fast-drawn artist a relaxed, reflective manner — and is his talent deceiving me, or is Wilder getting more attractive with the years?"

While Mel Brooks may never win any awards for good taste, he and his co-writers did win the Writers Guild of America Award for Best Comedy Written Directly for the Screen. In addition, *Blazing Saddles* received three Academy Award nominations, for Best Film Editing (John C. Howard and Danford Greene), Best Supporting Actress (Kahn), and Best Original Song (for the whip-cracking title tune sung by Frankie Laine, for which John Morris did the music and Brooks wrote the lyrics). Gene's performance went unnoticed, though in the film it is Harvey Korman who actually talks about his chances of being nominated for Best Supporting Actor.

Gene did, however, receive an Oscar nomination for his film work in 1974, this time for the screenplay of *Young Frankenstein*, which he co-wrote with Brooks. The idea for *Young Frankenstein* came to Gene one winter in Westhampton, New York. "One afternoon, at 2 o'clock," he recalled, "I took a long, yellow, legal pad and a black, felt pen — it may have been blue, but I think it was black — and wrote at the top of the page *Young Frankenstein*. And I proceeded to answer a few questions about what might happen to me in the present day if I were left Frankenstein's estate."

"I called Mel and told him the idea," Gene said, but Brooks seemed less than enthusiastic, saying only, "Cute, that's cute." Shortly thereafter, Gene's agent, Mike Medavoy, called him and said, "How about we make a picture with you, Peter Boyle and Marty Feldman?"

"How'd you come to that idea?" Gene asked him.

"Because I now represent you and Peter and Marty!"

"Well, that's a wonderful artistic basis for a film," Gene shot back, "and it so happens I do have something."

A few days later, Gene sent Medavoy a scene from *Young Franken-stein*. He loved it and suggested having Mel Brooks direct. "You're whistling 'Dixie,'" Gene said, "because Mel won't direct something he didn't conceive of." The next day, Brooks phoned Gene and said, "What are you getting me into?"

Gene wrote the entire first draft of the script, and then he and Brooks wrote several more drafts before filming began. The story involves Dr. Frederick Frankenstein, grandson of the infamous Dr. Victor Frankenstein, who is so ashamed of his grandfather that he insists on pronouncing his name *Fronkensteen*. After being presented with the will of his great grandfather, Baron Beaufort von Frankenstein, Frederick journeys to Transylvania. When he arrives at his family's ancestral castle, he encounters a number of oddballs: Igor (pronounced "Eye-gore"), a bug-eyed hunchback played by Marty Feldman in a career-defining performance; Inga, Frederick's sexy Swedish lab assistant, played by Teri Garr; and Cloris Leachman as Frau Blucher, the housekeeper whose name incites horses to whinny out of control. (*Blucher*, despite an early rumor perhaps perpetrated by Brooks himself, is *not* the German word for glue.)

While at the castle, Frederick stumbles upon a book by his grandfather detailing how he brought his creature to life. Freder-ick now becomes obsessed with creating his own creature, and with Igor and Inga's help, gets a hold of a fresh corpse and the brain of a deceased genius. There's only one problem — Igor dropped the brain Frederick wanted, so, not wanting to return to the laboratory empty-handed, Igor provides Frederick with another brain that was labeled "abnormal." This leads to what Gene has said is his favorite scene in the film where, after the newly animated creature nearly chokes Frederick to death, he asks Igor whose brain he used:

IGOR
*Abby someone.*
FREDDY
*Abby someone? Abby who?*
IGOR
*Abby Normal.*

In addition to parodying Mary Shelley's book and the first *Frankenstein* movie from 1931, Brooks and Wilder also use 1935's *Bride of Frankenstein* for source material, most notably by having the monster nearly killed by the hospitality of a blind hermit (Gene Hackman in a hilarious cameo).

On a technical level, the film is clearly Mel Brooks' best. Brooks and Wilder insisted on filming in black and white at a time when studios were strongly opposed to doing so because it would hurt sales to television and Europe. Brooks stood firm, though, and said if he couldn't shoot the movie in black and white, he would quit. As a result, thanks to Gerald Hirschfeld's moody lighting and camerawork and the actual lab equipment from James Whale's original *Frankenstein* movie that Kenneth Strickfaden let Brooks use, *Young Frankenstein* actually looks just like the films it is parodying.

It was during the making of *Young Frankenstein* that Gene Wilder and Mel Brooks had their first of only two fights (the second would occur more than thirty years later and also involve *Young Frankenstein*). Gene insisted on having a scene where he and the monster do a musical number in which they perform "Puttin' on the Ritz." Brooks thought it was a lousy idea and the two argued for days. "I was close to rage and tears," Gene said. Finally, Brooks relented and agreed to do the scene, much to Gene's surprise. "You're timid and you're shy and you don't fight for much," Brooks told him, "and if you fight that hard for something, there must be something good there." So good, in fact, that the "Puttin' on the Ritz" number remains one of the most famous scenes in the film.

Brooks and Wilder brought *Young Frankenstein* to Columbia Pictures, but they turned the project down, citing that the proposed budget was too high. Twentieth Century-Fox ultimately agreed to do the film and in the process signed both Wilder and Brooks to exclusive acting, writing, producing, and directing contracts. *Young Frankenstein* cost $2.8 million to make and grossed $40 million in its initial release, a substantial amount of money for 1974. The film was so popular that many movie theaters around the country held showings around the clock.

The film also tickled the critics. Pauline Kael wrote in *The New Yorker* that *Young Frankenstein* is "what used to be called a crazy comedy, and there hasn't been this kind of craziness on the screen in years. It's a film to go to when your rhythm is slowed down and you're too tired to think. You can't bring anything to it (Brooks's timing is too obvious for that); you have to let it do everything for you, because that's the only way it works. It has some of the obviousness of *Abbott & Costello Meet Frankenstein*, and if you go expecting too much it could seem like kids' stuff — which, of course, it is, but it's very funny kids' stuff..." For Gene, Kael had nothing but praise. "As a hysteric," she wrote, "he's funnier even than Peter Sellers. For Sellers, hysteria is just one more weapon in his comic arsenal — his hysteria mocks hysteria — but Wilder's hysteria seems perfectly natural. You never question what's driving him to it; his fits are lucid and total. They take him into a different dimension — he delivers what Harpo promised." And of his screenwriting, Kael noted that Gene "has a healthy respect for his own star abilities. Confidence seems to be making him better-looking with each picture; this time he wears a romantic, droopy mustache, and in full-face, with his eyes outlined and his long chin prominent, he gives a vain, John Barrymore-ish dash to the role."

Stanley Kauffmann was in a definite minority when he panned the film in *The New Republic*, saying it was "like a sketch from the old Sid Caesar show, for which Brooks wrote, spun out ten times as long. Ten times too long. Brooks is a sprinter, and there aren't enough good sprints here."

*Young Frankenstein* received Golden Globe nominations for Cloris Leachman (Best Actress in a Motion Picture — Musical or Comedy) and Madeline Kahn (Best Supporting Actress in a Motion Picture), a Writers Guild of America nomination for Best Comedy Adapted from Another Medium, and Oscar nominations for Best Sound (Richard Portman and Gene Cantamessa) and Best Screenplay Adapted from Other Material, but Wilder and Brooks lost to Francis Ford Coppola and Mario Puzo for *The Godfather Part II*, which swept the awards that year.

Gene Wilder acknowledges *Young Frankenstein* as his best film, saying, "Of all of the films, *Young Frankenstein* is the one that came the closest to realizing what *the intent* was — it was the way I wrote it." Gene has also called making *Young Frankenstein* "the happiest

film experience I've ever had." In fact, it was such a positive experience for him that he didn't want it to end. On the last day of filming,
Gene recalled, "I was terribly sad. I didn't want to leave Transylvania — the world we'd created and written for." Brooks saw Gene
was upset about something.

"Gene, what is it?" Brooks asked him. "I got setups to do, lighting…"

"I want us to write more scenes," Gene said.

"For what?"

"For this."

"Why?"

"Because I don't want to go home."

"Yeah, that's lovely, but we've run out of story and characters…
maybe if you could talk to Mary Shelley, who wrote the original" —
and who had been dead for more than a century.

Gene's portrayal of Dr. Frederick Frankenstein was ranked as the
ninth greatest film performance of all time by *Premiere* magazine
in a 2006 list of the 100 greatest film performances, both male and
female. He was sandwiched below James Stewart in *It's a Wonderful
Life* (1946) at #8 and above Robert DeNiro in *Raging Bull* (1980)
at #10.

Despite Gene's chemistry with Madeline Kahn, he said, when
addressing an audience of UCLA film students in 1976, "Madeline
is not now or has ever been my girlfriend, but I believe I know her
talent as an actress better than anyone else." While Gene's relationship with Kahn was platonic, his relationship with Teri Garr was
not. During the making of *Young Frankenstein*, the two got along
particularly well.

"She was fresh and funny and sexy, and Gene was absolutely
crazy about her," Brooks said. "And…they liked each other a lot.
That's all I'll say."

As was the case with their characters in the film, there was a
definite romantic spark offscreen. After filming was completed, the
two began dating around the same time Gene was finalizing his
divorce from Jo. The relationship was not long lasting, however,
though Gene maintained they continued to be "good pals" after
the romance ended.

"I love directing. I'd rather direct than act or write."

— *Gene Wilder*

# 7

# Auteur! Auteur!

While they were editing *Young Frankenstein*, Mel Brooks gave Gene Wilder a lot of filmmaking advice. "After the picture was shot," remembers Gene, "Mel and I spent five days a week for four months in this tiny little screening room and he was telling me things like, 'Don't make that mistake. Make sure you cover enough on the closeup [sic] so you can always correct a mistake, save a scene.' I used to say, 'Why are you telling me this?' And he would say, 'You'll see, if you go on writing, it'll happen soon enough.' He meant that if you go on writing, you're going to want to protect your scripts. And that you'll be a director because you have the talent or you'll fall on your ass and never get another picture. But you'll get your shot."

In 1975 Gene got all of the shots he wanted when he made what seemed like the inevitable progression to auteur, following in the footsteps of his mentor Mel. The film was *The Adventure of Sherlock Holmes' Smarter Brother*, which Gene wrote, directed, and starred in. Gene had always been fond of Arthur Conan Doyle's detective stories, and after discussing the possibility of a Sherlock spoof with his friend, producer Richard A. Roth, Gene came up with the idea of Sherlock having a jealous younger brother who thinks he's really the smarter one.

*The Adventure of Sherlock Holmes' Smarter Brother* was the first screenplay Gene wrote entirely on his own. He had been writing since 1968, when he came up with an idea for a comedy about a spy in World War I that he was going to call *Hesitation Waltz*. He solicited the help of his old friend Jane Fonda, with whom he used to play Parker Brothers board games as a young actor in New York. Fonda brought the story to the attention of Francois Truffaut, who informed Gene that he had no interest in directing a film in English. So nothing became of *Hesitation Waltz* until 2007 when Gene used it as the basis for his first published work of fiction, *My French Whore*. Years later, Gene confessed he desperately wanted to work with Truffaut and sent the French director numerous notes requesting a meeting. "If he ever worked with me," Gene said, "it would be because he wanted someone who was funny and sad at the same time. That would appeal to him, I'm sure." *

For *The Adventure of Sherlock Holmes' Smarter Brother*, Gene assembled the key members of Mel Brooks' stock company: Madeline Kahn, Marty Feldman, Dom DeLuise, and, of course, himself. As he would go on to direct, Gene would continue to use many of the same cast and crew, some of whom were also good friends. Gene directed Dom DeLuise in three of the four films they appeared in together. John Morris, who has done the music for most of Mel Brooks' movies, has done the music for four of Gene's films as a director (the exception being his segment of *Sunday Lovers*). The late Chris Greenbury was Gene's favorite editor. Gerald Hirschfeld and Fred Schuler are his choice cinematographers. He even gave one of his closest relatives, his late cousin Mark "Buddy" Silberman, small parts in *The World's Greatest Lover* and *The Woman in Red*. Working with friends makes for a special camaraderie on the set, as Madeline Kahn was able to attest to. She said working on *Sherlock* was the most enjoyable experience she'd ever had making a movie. "It was put together like needlepoint, much more carefully than most movies," she said. "For me, it was especially fun since I was working with my friends."

---

* Interestingly, Truffaut was the first choice to direct *Bonnie and Clyde*, but he turned it down to make *Fahrenheit 451* (1966) instead.

In the film, Gene plays Sigerson Holmes, the younger brother of the world's most famous crime solver, who agrees to take over one of Sherlock's cases while he's out of the country. His assignment is to protect dance hall girl Jenny Hill (Kahn), who is being blackmailed by a rotund opera star named Eduardo Gambetti (DeLuise). Feldman plays Sigerson's right-hand man Orville Sacker, who has a photographic sense of hearing that more or less makes him a human tape recorder. (Gene's affection for Conan Doyle's work is evident to Holmes historians who know that Orville Sacker was Conan Doyle's original name for Dr. Watson and that Sigerson was an alias Sherlock used after his struggle at Reichenbach Falls.)

Upon the film's release, obvious comparisons were made between Gene Wilder and Mel Brooks. Having worked so closely with Brooks, much of his comic sensibility rubbed off on Gene, yet their approaches are different. Whereas Brooks gets laughs by hitting his audience on the head with a sledgehammer, Gene achieves the same result using a Q-tip. Among the similarities between Wilder and Brooks, however, is their fondness for injecting musical numbers into their narrative. For Brooks, they often remain the one thing about his films people most remember. And Gene would go on to include them in his films as well. In *Sherlock*, Sigerson, Jenny, and Orville suddenly burst into the whimsical strains of "The Kangaroo Hop," a bouncy tune filled with Gene's delightfully cornball lyrics ("If you're over eighty you can waltz a little while/But hopping around the parlor is the very latest style…"). And then there are the Gay Nineties style songs Jenny sings at the Tivoli Music Hall, as well as Gene's daffy staging of Verdi's opera *The Masked Ball*.

Some have accused Gene of not daring to go all out in terms of naughtiness the way that Brooks does. Yet there are some scenes in *Sherlock* that contradict this belief. Most notable is arguably the film's funniest scene in which Sigerson and Orville, dressed in white tie and tails, narrowly escape being sawed in half by a huge rotating blade. They wander into a cotillion and proceed to dance with two ladies, unaware that while they didn't get sawed to pieces, the seats of their trousers did. Had the Marx Brothers been able to show their posteriors on film, this likely would have been the result.

Gene's gentler style was welcomed by many critics, among them *The Washington Post*'s Gary Arnold, who enjoyed Gene's "relatively subtle, ironic touch, which recalls the eccentric style of British film comedy." Derek Malcolm of *The Guardian* did not agree, however, finding Gene's approach "less frenetic...not so likely to bruise us half to death in the name of laughter. But it also lacks Brooks' bludgeoning energy, which can transform a comic set piece into a tour de force." On the whole, the critics were generous, though. *Time* magazine's Richard Schickel called it "the fastest escape from the blahs Hollywood is offering this season," while Judith Crist found it to be "a comedy of wit and imagination" and wrote in the *Saturday Review*, "Kahn and Wilder, never better in performance, carry the day with good humor." Most kind, however, was *The New York Times*' Vincent Canby, who wrote, "Gene Wilder makes an impressive debut as a comedy director" and that the film is "full of affection and generous feelings for the genre it's having fun with." Canby went on to call *Sherlock* "a charming slapstick comedy that honors Sir Arthur Conan Doyle's original creation as much by what it doesn't do as by what it does do. The film is a marvelously lowbrow caper but it makes no attempt to parody the great Sherlock himself, who is treated with cheerful if distant awe and respect, measured entirely in terms of Sigerson's ineptitude."

In a 1984 article on first-time directors, writer Jeff Rovin differed considerably with the critics who in 1975 praised Gene's directorial debut. He wrote in *Video Movies* magazine that "the group that consistently makes the worst first films are actors. Because most are stars, they have seen their performances undermined by bad dialogue. Not surprisingly, when they're first handed the directorial responsibility, they're determined to make the star look good. And considering that the star of their first film is most often themselves, the results are usually disastrous...

"In the category of worst performance by a first-time director, Gene Wilder takes the gold for *The Adventure of Sherlock Holmes' Smarter Brother* (1975). Dizzy enough under any director, Wilder, left to his own devices, is unbearably loud and silly as he strives to protect dancehall girl Madeline Kahn from danger. Co-stars Kahn, Marty Feldman, and Dom DeLuise are also infected by Wilder's overacting bug, though Albert Finney's unbilled cameo as a theatergoer is a gem."

Gene Wilder has received his fair share of negative reviews, but he tries not to let them get him down. He has very little regard for film critics, though Pat Collins is a friend, as was Joel Siegel. Gene feels that film criticism is "all subjective" and that the critics "don't know anything about movies anyway." "There are very few critics in this country," Gene said in 1979. "There are many, many reviewers and that's more honest. Gene Shalit, for instance. He doesn't pretend to be a critic. He's like my Aunt Tillie." Gene proceeded to imitate Shalit's voice. "'Ohh, I loved it. It was wonderful. You're going to laugh. My stomach ached.'"

While he realizes the importance of critics and wants his films to be hits that audiences enjoy, he has said that self-satisfaction is just as important to him. In a 1986 interview with Barbara Howar, Gene said, "I know at this point in my life that I'm never going to please everyone…If you're not doing it to satisfy yourself, then who are you doing it for? You're doing it to satisfy the most people in the world that you can. I'm not trying to say that I don't want people to laugh if I do something funny in a movie. But I'm saying I want them to laugh — hopefully — but most of all I want to say I like what I did."

After *The Adventure of Sherlock Holmes' Smarter Brother*, Gene Wilder would go on to direct three more feature films and one segment of another — a total of 4½ in Fellini terms — in between acting in other people's films, meeting with both success and failure, as well as occasional self-satisfaction.

# 8

# A Winning Streak

Despite the enormous success of *Blazing Saddles*, film buffs still wonder how different a film it would have been if Richard Pryor had been cast as the sheriff. The consensus is that Cleavon Little was very good but that Pryor would have taken the film to comic heights unimaginable. It also would have teamed Gene Wilder and Richard Pryor together on-screen. But it didn't happen. Two years later, however, Wilder and Pryor did get to work together in *Silver Streak*, and the result was one of Gene Wilder's most successful movies.

Of course, Gene was a director now, but unlike Woody Allen or Mel Brooks, who only occasionally appeared in another director's film, Gene mostly acted in other people's films while only sporadically directing.

*Silver Streak* was written by Colin Higgins, who up to this point was best known for *Harold and Maude* (1972) and would go on to write and direct *Nine to Five* (1980) and *The Best Little Whorehouse in Texas* (1982). Higgins had always loved Alfred Hitchcock's classic *North by Northwest* (1959) and wanted to write a script that would be an homage to that film.

Executive producer Martin Ransohoff felt that Arthur Hiller, with whom he had done *The Wheeler Dealers* (1963) and *The*

*Americanization of Emily* (1964), would be the best choice to direct the film. "He said, 'Arthur, I've got your next picture. Come over, pick it up and take it home and read it now!'" recalled Hiller. "And when he gave it to me, he said, 'Now go home and read it now! Don't wait! Let me know right away. Because this is for you and this is perfect.' And on page thirty-two I phoned and I said, 'Marty, you're right. I'll do the picture.'"

From the beginning, Gene was thought of to play the lead. While he was editing *The Adventure of Sherlock Holmes' Smarter Brother* in Paris, Gene received a call from his good friend, Alan Ladd, Jr. Ladd was head of production at Twentieth Century-Fox and was responsible for giving *Young Frankenstein* the go-ahead. He told Gene about *Silver Streak* and said he would need to know if Gene wanted to do it by Sunday (Ladd had called him on a Friday). Ladd put the script on a plane and had someone personally deliver it to Gene. Three hours after receiving it, Gene called Los Angeles with his acceptance. "It was the best film script that I'd read since *Blazing Saddles*," he said. His affinity for Ladd and Fox was apparent. "Another studio wouldn't get the same speedy reply," Gene said.

*Silver Streak* opens with Gene as George Caldwell, a mild-mannered book editor, boarding a luxury train from Los Angeles to Chicago, where he is going to attend his sister's wedding. George's cabin on the train connects to another room, but, due to a faulty latch, he accidentally opens the connecting door as Hilly Burns (Jill Clayburgh) is dressing.

As George's train journey begins, he meets a boisterous vitamin salesman named Bob Sweet (Ned Beatty), who freely dispenses samples of vitamin E. During dinner, Hilly asks George if she may join him, and after enough martinis and champagne, a romance develops. As George and Hilly are in their room getting intimate, George sees a dead body fall from the train. Hilly convinces him it was probably nothing, a result of all the champagne they had been drinking. The next morning, George sees a picture of Hilly's boss, a professor who has just written a book on Rembrandt, and tells her that that's the man he saw fall off the train. She tells him to go down the hall to the professor's room and see for himself that he is all right. When George goes to the professor's room, however, he is greeted by a little thug (Ray Walston) and thrown off the train by a giant with bad dental work named Reace (Richard Kiel).

George eventually manages to get back on the train, but it's already too late, for Hilly has now taken up company with hotshot jet-setter Roger Devereau (Patrick McGoohan). When George tells Bob Sweet of his encounter with Reace, Sweet starts asking George a series of questions that leads Sweet to tell George he is really a federal agent trailing Devereau for his involvement in a major art forgery. After Sweet is shot dead by Reace, George becomes the suspect and once again manages to fall off the train, but now he's wanted for murder.

George fears for Hilly's safety, but when he goes to a hick sheriff (Clifton James) to tell him the truth, George winds up turning the tables on the sheriff and stealing his patrol car to try getting back on the Silver Streak to save Hilly. In the back of the patrol car is Grover T. Muldoon (Pryor), a thief who helps George outwit the police.

Probably the most famous scene from *Silver Streak* occurs in a train station men's room where Grover, trying to disguise George so he can pass by the police and get back on the train, rubs shoe polish on George's face in an attempt to make him pass for black. Though Wilder and Pryor adhered for the most part to Higgins' script, Hiller allowed them the freedom to ad-lib, such as when Pryor says to Wilder, "What, are you afraid it won't come off?" "That's a good joke," Gene ad-libs back. "That's humorous."

"We were worried about that scene, that it might hurt people's feelings," Gene told Roger Ebert in an interview he and Pryor gave for the *Chicago Sun-Times*. "The way it was written, after I disguise myself, a white man is fooled by my disguise. That was bad, because then we'd be saying blacks were like that. And so Richie came up with a brilliant structural change, and the scene gets one of the biggest laughs in the movie."

Pryor picked up where Gene left off. "Instead of a white dude being fooled by the disguise, a black dude comes in and *isn't* fooled," Pryor said. "Here's Gene snapping his fingers and holding his portable radio to his ear, and the black dude takes one look and says, 'I don't know what you think you're doing, man, but you got to get the *beat*.'"

Though in the film the Silver Streak makes its journey from Los Angeles to Chicago, the movie was actually filmed in Canada using the Canadian Pacific Railroad because the Canadian landscape offered scenic snowcapped mountains, deserts, and prairies that couldn't be found with any U.S. railroad. For the film's ending — in which the runaway train crashes through Chicago's Union Station — Hiller and his production designer worked hard trying to figure out how to realistically shoot the train crash. They ultimately decided to do it full-scale using a hangar at the Burbank Airport which was recreated to look like Union Station. Hiller cut in shots of people running in Toronto's train station and some actual shots of Chicago's station, which editor David Bretherton seamlessly put together for the film's grand finale.

The film required a lot of stunts, including one dangerous one that Wilder and Pryor performed themselves in which Wilder hangs out of the runaway train while Pryor holds on to his belt. They rehearsed the scene at ten miles per hour but filmed it at fifty miles per hour. Pryor promised Gene that if he fell off the train and was killed, Pryor would throw himself off after him.

Although Gene got along well with Pryor, he was unaware that Pryor was less than thrilled making the film. According to Pryor biographer Jim Haskins, "in the course of filming *Silver Streak*, he had come to resent his very involvement in the film. He'd decided that the *Silver Streak* brass had brought him in primarily to prevent criticism from blacks. At some point something had snapped inside Pryor's supersensitive soul, and he stood back and looked at himself having a good time playing second-fiddle to Gene Wilder in a film in which he didn't even make his first appearance until halfway through the story..."

*Silver Streak* was released on December 3, 1976 and went on to become one of the year's biggest hits, grossing over $50 million. "In box office terms," Hiller said, "when it came out it did okay the first week...and then it went up the second weekend, which is unusual — it usually drops the second weekend — and then it went up even more the third weekend, so the word of mouth obviously was very good."

*Silver Streak* was nominated for an Academy Award for Best Sound (Don Mitchell, Douglas Williams, Richard Tyler, and

Hal Etherington), a Writers Guild of America Award for Best Comedy Written Directly for the Screen, and earned Gene his second Golden Globe nomination for Best Actor in a Motion Picture — Musical or Comedy (he lost to Kris Kristofferson in *A Star Is Born*).

Though *Silver Streak* opened to mixed reviews, it is now considered a classic, and the scene in which George and Hilly first make love in their connecting room has even been singled out in Syd Field's screenwriting book as an example of how to write a well-constructed romantic comedy scene.

Gene followed *Silver Streak* with his second outing as a director, *The World's Greatest Lover*, which was the last film he did while under contract to Twentieth Century-Fox. Set in the 1920s, when silent films were still all the rage, the film concerns Rudy Hickman, a Milwaukee baker who suffers from such tics as sticking his tongue out at people when he gets nervous. Fed up with his humdrum life, he decides to move to Hollywood with his wife Annie (Carol Kane), change his name to Rudy Valentine, and try out for a contest to become the next Rudolph Valentino.

Gene first approached Madeline Kahn to play Annie, but Kahn felt she wasn't right for the part and suggested Carol Kane. Gene knew Kane had been in *Carnal Knowledge* (1971) and *Dog Day Afternoon* (1975), but he hadn't seen those films. He had Twentieth Century-Fox set up a screening of *Hester Street*, the 1975 film for which Kane was nominated for a Best Actress Oscar, and after the screening Gene knew he wanted her. "She's a misfit," Gene said. "She's beautiful. She's simple. She can be plain or mistaken as plain. She can be ravishing — but most of all, she has fantasies in her heart that long to be expressed and that show themselves mostly with a frightened twinkle in her eye."

The idea for *The World's Greatest Lover* began taking shape after Gene finished making *The Adventure of Sherlock Holmes' Smarter Brother*. "It was Christmas time," Gene told *Newsday*'s Leo Seligsohn. "I had just gotten back from London and was living in a rented house in California and trying to think of a way to hold together the technical people that I had used in *Sherlock*. I started the way

I always do, with the magic 'if.' Stanislavsky said, 'Ask yourself the question, What would you do *if*…What would happen *if* Holmes had an extremely jealous younger brother?…What would happen *if* a neurotic baker followed his compulsive dreams of fame and romance to Hollywood…?"

Gene allowed himself to do the kind of physical slapstick comedy that is rarely seen these days. In one of the film's early scenes, Rudy, working on a bakery assembly line in which he must decorate cakes passing by, is daydreaming. When he awakens, he winds up getting covered in icing and sequins and having his head boxed and tied with a ribbon in a scene that Gene has said is a tribute to Charlie Chaplin in *Modern Times* (1936). Gene considers Chaplin his "greatest influence" and regards him as his patron saint and spiritual father. Along with Mervyn LeRoy's *Random Harvest* (1942), Chaplin's *City Lights* (1931) is Gene's favorite film of all time.

In addition to writing, directing, acting, and once again writing a song, Gene also served as producer of *The World's Greatest Lover*. Terence Marsh and Chris Greenbury co-produced (Greenbury also wrote the novelization published by Ace Books). "I don't want to produce anymore," Gene said after the film came out. "I want the artistic control but I don't want the headaches, the administrative headaches…I'm going to do in the future what Woody Allen does now. You have to have someone that you trust completely who handles all of the administrative problems but does not wish to be a writer, secretly. Someone who does not wish to be a director, secretly. Someone who respects your talent as you respect his or her talent as a producer and they make all the administrative decisions, the money decisions."

*The World's Greatest Lover* opened on December 18, 1977. Vincent Canby of *The New York Times* called it "frequently side splitting" and observed, "For a comedy of this kind, *The World's Greatest Lover* is uncommonly handsome, the period sets and costumes having a lot of the fantasy quality of a stylish Broadway musical. There are also times when the film's action seems to have been choreographed, which suggests the flow of a musical as well as the movements of old time slapstick farce. Thus even when one isn't laughing, one is ᵊguiled."

Gene admitted that his inspiration for *The World's Greatest Lover* came from Federico Fellini's 1951 film *The White Sheik*. Although not a shot-by-shot remake, there are enough similarities between the two films to consider *The World's Greatest Lover* more than just an homage to *The White Sheik*. At the very least, it is a "loose" remake. Wanting to avoid any legal trouble or be accused of ripping off Fellini's film, Gene contacted Fellini personally. The two had a phone conversation in which Fellini told Gene not to worry. All Fellini asked was that Gene thank him in the end credits. So the finished film boasts a full-screen tribute that reads, "A loving thank you from Gene Wilder to his friend, Federico Fellini, for encouragement at just the right time."

*"He came from the old Bar Mitzvah spread*
*With a 10-gallon yarmulke on his head*
*He always followed his mother's wishes*
*Even on the range he used two sets of dishes."*

— "The Ballad of Irving"*

* A 1966 novelty song by Frank Peppiatt, John Aylesworth, and Dick Williams, performed by Frank Gallop.

# 9

# A Kosher Cowboy

Gene's next film was to have paired him with a bona fide screen legend, John Wayne. Wayne had actually been approached by Mel Brooks at one point to play Gene's role in *Blazing Saddles*, but, although Wayne thought the script was hilarious, he turned Brooks down, telling him, "I can't do this! This is too dirty! I'm John Wayne!"

Originally called *No Knife*, the film's title, which no one seemed to like, was changed to *The Frisco Kid* shortly before being released (though there had been a 1935 James Cagney film called *Frisco Kid*, producer Mace Neufeld obtained a waiver from the MPAA allowing him to use the title).*

The film tells the story of a naive rabbi from Poland who travels to America in the 1850s to lead a congregation in San Francisco. Neufeld had optioned the script for *No Knife* in 1975 and at one point Mike Nichols, Milos Forman, and Bud Yorkin were all interested in directing. Robert Aldrich, known for such gritty fare as *The Dirty Dozen* (1967) and *The Longest Yard* (1974), ultimately got the

---

* Several of Gene Wilder's film titles were also titles of older films. There was a 1934 feature called *The Silver Streak*, as well as a 1945 animated short with the same title; the 1935 film *The Rainmakers* was originally called *The Silver Streak*; *The Haunted Honeymoon* was a 1925 short; the 1940 film *Busman's Honeymoon* was also known as *Haunted Honeymoon*; *The Woman in Red* was a 1935 Barbara Stanwyck drama; and *The Lady in Question* was the name of a 1940 Rita Hayworth film.

job. For the lead, Dustin Hoffman was thought of early on to play the rabbi, as was Henry Winkler. The script was eventually sent to Gene's agent and Gene agreed to do the film.

Steve Martin heard about the script and very much wanted to play the part of the bank robber who ends up showing the rabbi the ways of the West, but Warner Bros. had no interest in Martin. The script was sent to Wayne's agent and Wayne loved the part. Gene's contract called for him to get first billing, but if Wayne came onboard, he would insist on top billing. Gene was so excited at the prospect of working with Wayne that he had no problem at all with his name coming second.

It was no secret that Wayne was not in the best of health, so it was thought this might be his final film. Wayne backed out of the project shortly before filming was to begin, not because of illness, though, but because of a disagreement over money after a Warner Bros. executive went to Wayne's home and tried to talk him into accepting a $750,000 salary instead of the $1 million he was initially promised. Harrison Ford, who had recently rose to prominence as Han Solo in *Star Wars* (1977), was Wayne's significantly younger last-minute replacement. Ford got the role thanks to Henry Winkler, who had worked with him on a film called *Heroes* (1977), and suggested Ford would be ideal for the part.

As Avram Belinski, Gene gave one of his most nuanced performances as the bearded rabbi with a heavy accent whose heart is perhaps a little bigger than his brain. Shortly after arriving in America, Avram is beaten up and robbed. It is the kindness of Tommy Lillard (Ford), an outlaw who takes pity on Avram, that helps the rabbi on his journey.

Gene put much effort into preparing for his role. "Gene was an absolute perfect ten as a comedy actor," Neufeld said. "He worked very hard on the religious part of the part. I got two rabbis in as advisors and a cantor who taught him to chant. Gene was very, very serious about that."

Part of the film was shot in Rio Rico, Colorado. At the same time, director Hal Needham was there filming *The Villain* (1979) with Kirk Douglas, Ann-Margret, and Arnold Schwarzenegger. Because there was only one hotel in the area, both movie companies occupied it, and on the Fourth of July, they had one big party, giving Gene a chance to reminisce with Douglas about working together on Broadway fifteen years earlier.

Gene got along well with Ford and the two would often have dinner at a local pub after the day's shooting ended. One day during filming, Gene mentioned to Ford that he had gone to the Black-Foxe Military Institute. Ford, a skilled carpenter, told Gene that he had bought the floorboards after Black-Foxe was torn down. While Gene is obviously Jewish and played a very Jewish role in the film, Ford himself is half-Jewish on his mother's side (which, according to Jewish law, makes him Jewish). "[A]t one point," Gene remembered, "during some conversation, Harrison said, 'Why do you say that? I'm half-Jewish.' He certainly didn't seem Jewish."

Though Michael Elias and Frank Shaw are credited with writing *The Frisco Kid*, Gene was asked to collaborate on the third draft of the script and then rewrote much of the fourth draft but, because a screenplay credit was not in his contract, did not receive on-screen billing.

Aldrich enjoyed working with Gene, and told *Films and Filming* magazine, "Gene is brilliant. I think it's the best job he's ever done." Unfortunately for Ford, Aldrich never got over losing John Wayne, and his resentment towards Ford was apparent. "Even though it was his final choice to cast Harrison," Neufeld recalled, "I think that every time the camera rolled and he was looking at Harrison, he was picturing John Wayne. And Harrison, I think, was quite aware of that."

Warner Bros. executives were disappointed in *The Frisco Kid* and therefore didn't invest a lot of money on a proper marketing campaign. The film opened on July 13, 1979 to mixed reviews. It cost $10 million to make and grossed about the same amount at the box office, though *Daily Variety* wrote, "Gene Wilder has his best role in years. The manic gleam in the earlier Wilder pix has now turned into a mature twinkle, and this performance is particularly impressive in accumulation of small character details." Julian Fox of *Films and Filming* magazine called Gene's performance "Oscar-worthy" and the film a western "head and shoulders above anything I have seen in a long time."

# 10

# "That's Right! We Baaaad!"

In 1980 Gene Wilder went to prison — but it was for a good reason. Capitalizing on their rapport in *Silver Streak*, Gene and Richard Pryor were once again paired together, this time in equal roles, for *Stir Crazy*. Bruce Jay Friedman's screenplay was at one point offered to Arthur Hiller, who would have loved to again work with his *Silver Streak* stars, but felt that he wasn't the right director for the project. Sidney Poitier, who during this period was concentrating solely on directing, ended up making the film (he had previously directed Pryor in the 1974 comedy *Uptown Saturday Night*).

*Stir Crazy*, which was first going to be called *Prison Rodeo*, then *Jailbirds*, opens in New York with Gene singing "Crazy" — not the Patsy Cline song — over the opening credits sequence. Wilder and Pryor play Skip Donahue and Harry Monroe. Skip is a playwright, Harry an actor. They both are having no luck in their individual careers and pay the bills by working as a department store detective and waiter, respectively.

After they are both fired, Skip convinces Harry that they should abandon New York and move out West. They find work as singing woodpeckers, doing a song and dance routine in a bank. But things go horribly awry when two thugs steal Skip and Harry's woodpecker costumes and rob the bank. Now the police think it was Skip and Harry who pulled the bank job, and the two are sentenced to 125 years in a state penitentiary. Their only hope is to pull off an elaborate escape plan during a prison rodeo in which Skip, who has a hidden talent for riding bulls, is participating.

Skip Donahue is in many ways the quintessential Gene Wilder performance. He manages to intersperse his two personas — calm and soft-spoken and raving lunatic — flawlessly, such as in the scene where he and Pryor are being escorted in a prison line to their cell. After being hit in the stomach by a guard, Gene proceeds to freak out, doing everything from spitting on the guard's belt, riding him like a horse, and acting like a squirrel. Teamwork is truly defined as Pryor restores him to sanity, only to need him to do the same for him when he begins to lose it.

The character of Skip Donahue is the ultimate goody-two-shoes, a naive peacemaker who believes everyone's intentions are honest and good. It's easy to imagine that if Felix Unger and Edith Bunker were to have a son, Skip Donahue may have been him. Skip always looks to break up a fight, such as in one of the film's early scenes in a bar where a cabbie is being bullied by a customer who just stiffed him. "All those two fellows need is someone to talk to them gently, with compassion," Skip tells Harry. "That's all that they need." Later on in prison, when he attempts to make friends with a hulking mass murderer named Grossberger, Gene brings to mind the scene in *Young Frankenstein* where he insists on being locked up with the monster to convince him that he is loved.

*Stir Crazy* went into production in February of 1980. Most of the prison scenes were shot in the Arizona State Penitentiary in Florence, near Tucson, while other scenes were filmed on a soundstage in Burbank. Both Wilder and Pryor, along with the rest of the cast and crew, were required to sign forms which stated, "I understand that in the event I should be taken hostage or involved in a disturbance, institution authorities will not be expected to make extraordinary or unusual effort to effect my release."

Only once did Gene feel uneasy during the shoot. "There's a little scene in the movie where I was put into a metal hut for punishment..." he recalled. "We were shooting just below Death Row in a maximum security section, and the inmates were shouting the worst obscenities I've ever heard in my life. But they weren't shouting them at me, they were shouting them at Sidney; and when I heard the things directed at blacks coming from them, I started to shake a little bit. And Sidney [grabbed] me and said, 'Don't let that get to you, you just go about your business. You know who you are, you know who I am, and you know what we have to do!' And that gave me a lot of confidence in him, because he'd been through it before. I'd been through it in other ways, but not like that; not from people who had nothing to lose and just went crazy. They were already on Death Row, what else could they do to them."

Pryor took pride in ingratiating himself to the actual inmates by offering them soft drinks, and even admitted to sneaking them drugs. During filming, Pryor, whose drug abuse during this period was rampant, intentionally distanced himself from his fellow actors and crew members. Instead of staying at the luxury hotel where Wilder and Poitier were, Pryor opted for renting what he described as a "ramshackle home in the hills that was as isolated as I was trying to make myself."

Pryor's drug use resulted in him often showing up on the set late — sometimes half a day late — which infuriated the crew and delayed production to the point where the film's $10 million budget ballooned to $15 million. Pryor also had a series of confrontations with one of the cameramen, which came to a head when the cameraman accidentally threw a slice of watermelon at Pryor's feet during an impromptu game of "watermelon Frisbee." After that incident, Pryor walked off the set for a week. Pryor's unprofessional behavior upset Poitier so much that he met with Columbia Pictures executives and threatened to replace him with another actor and reshoot his early scenes. But Pryor ended up returning to finish the picture.

Gene took Pryor's behavioral problems in stride and didn't let it affect their relationship. "Gene is a very respectful person," said cinematographer Fred Schuler. "I guess, no matter what, he would never complain about Richard being late."

Though Wilder and Pryor were friendly during filming, they rarely ever saw each other off the set. However, Gene did visit Pryor in the hospital while he was recovering from severe burns suffered after setting himself on fire while freebasing cocaine several months after *Stir Crazy* finished principal photography.

*Stir Crazy* opened on December 12, 1980. Overall, critics gave the film mixed reviews. Joseph Gelmis had praise for it, writing in *Newsday*, "Wilder is a superb farceur, Pryor a first-rate writer and stand-up monologist. They have an affinity that brings out the best vibes in each other. They are accomplices, but civilized, not anti-social outlaws, in a barbaric world of criminals and corrupt lawmen. That bonding, and the gentleness of their relationship, is part of what makes their slapstick more than shtick. Their affinity is chemical. They share a state of mind, speak a common language." Gelmis concluded, "If Wilder and Pryor work for you, you'll enjoy their mellow tomfoolery in *Stir Crazy*. If they don't, you won't. Without them, the movie would be nothing."

Roger Ebert thought *Stir Crazy* got off to a great start, but wrote, "once Wilder and Pryor are thrown into prison, it seems to lose its way." Ebert also felt that "either Poitier or the producers made a tactical error in making Wilder the more aggressive character and Pryor the laid-back one. This is casting against type, all right: Wilder is brilliant at being meek and laid-back, and Pryor is a genius when he's allowed to be hyper. But it just doesn't feel right when Wilder goes for the high notes and Pryor hangs back."

Whatever critics may have had to say had little impact on *Stir Crazy*'s success. The film was a blockbuster hit, taking in over $100 million at the box office and becoming the third biggest money-maker of 1980 after *The Empire Strikes Back* and *Nine to Five*. In its first week in release, it grossed a then record $12 million, toppling records previously set by *Close Encounters of the Third Kind* (1977) and *Kramer vs. Kramer* (1979). It still remains Gene Wilder's highest-grossing film,* and, up until *Scary Movie* in 2000, the most profitable film ever directed by a black filmmaker. In addition, the

---

* With a total box office take of $101 million, *Stir Crazy* is Gene Wilder's highest-grossing film in terms of initial release. *Blazing Saddles*, which was rereleased several times after its February 1974 opening, actually grossed the most money of any of his films, taking in a lifetime total of $120 million.

ad-libbed scene in which Wilder and Pryor first go to jail and try to act "baaaad" quickly became a part of the American lexicon.

In 1985 CBS turned *Stir Crazy* into a TV series with a newcomer named Joseph Guzaldo playing Skip Donahue. Unlike the film, the show never found an audience and was quickly canceled.

Gene followed *Stir Crazy* with an obscure film released in 1981 called *Sunday Lovers*. The film was an attempt to show men dealing with romantic relationships in four different countries — England, France, Italy, and the United States. Each segment had a different director. Gene wrote, directed, and starred in the American segment titled "Skippy," in which he played a man who checks himself into a mental hospital in the hopes of curing a sexual problem. Kathleen Quinlan played Gene's love interest.

Gene jokingly described his segment as a "tastefully, semi-por-nographic love story." Leonard Maltin called Gene's contribution to the film "pretentious" and "embarrassingly bad." Vincent Canby of *The New York Times* found it "appalling," writing, "Mr. Wilder is a maddening talent, capable of marvelous work in films like Mel Brooks's 'Young Frankenstein,' his own 'Sherlock Holmes's Smarter Brother' and in Woody Allen's 'Everything You Ever Wanted to Know About Sex,' but he's not even tolerable in things like 'Stir Crazy' and this minor mess. His fatal weakness is to cast himself not simply as a love-object but as a love-object who is full of pathos."

For once, the negative reaction to Gene's work seemed justified, for even the biggest Gene Wilder fan would be hard-pressed to find anything redeeming about "Skippy." The only thing universal about *Sunday Lovers* — or *Les Seducteurs* as it was known in France — was that it was a universal flop.

"I've been married twice and both times to Catholic girls...I think the next time I'll be healthy enough to at least consider 'going out' with a Jewish girl!"

— *Gene Wilder*

# 11

# This Nice Jewish Girl from Detroit

The script was called *Traces*. It was a comic murder mystery in the tradition of Hitchcock that Gene Wilder wanted to do simply so he could once again work with his good friend Sidney Poitier. Gilda Radner, who had a year earlier left her star-making five-year run on *Saturday Night Live*, was cast as the woman Gene falls in love with in the film, which was retitled *Hanky Panky*. It didn't take long before their movie romance developed offscreen as well.

"I'd give it all up for love," Gilda once said of her career, and in Gene she had found someone who she described as "funny and athletic and handsome, and he smelled good." Never so much attracted to the good-looking guy so much as the funny one, Gilda confessed, "A funny man is irresistible. More than any looks, more than anything."

Ironically, Gene didn't look forward to working with "this nice Jewish girl from Detroit," as Gilda often characterized herself. In a 1986 interview he and Gilda did with Marilyn Beck, Gene said, "I thought this aggressive Detroit Jewish bitch was going to come on, improvise through every scene, [and] say, 'No, no, no, no. That's not how we do it on *Saturday Night Live*,' and push her way through. And this little timid girl comes on...She was just Miss Shy."

In addition to Gene expecting Gilda to be difficult, Gene was quite different than Gilda anticipated he would be. "She thought I was queer," Gene said, "because she saw *Stir Crazy* and she got it in her head that I was tutti-frutti. Just because Richard kissed me one time."

"After seeing his movies," Gilda admitted, "I thought, he's much taller than I ever thought. And much handsomer than I ever thought...And not as tutti-frutti as I thought."

Gene and Gilda's paths almost crossed before *Hanky Panky*. "She had seen my movies and I had seen her on television," Gene said. "But we never met until August 13, 1981, on the first night of shooting *Hanky Panky*. She says she saw me one time when I came to the NBC building to do an interview. She wanted to come over but felt uncomfortable about doing it. I wish she had."

There was one complication for Gene and Gilda's blossoming romance — Gilda was married. Her husband was musician G.E. Smith, who for years was the bandleader on *Saturday Night Live*. They were married a year and the marriage was already on the skids. Meeting Gene just confirmed for Gilda that the marriage was over. Gilda and Smith soon got an amicable divorce and remained on friendly terms. Prior to Smith, Gilda had been romantically involved with Peter Firth, Bill Murray, Chris Sarandon, and Kevin Kline.

*Hanky Panky* began production in August 1981 with a cast that included Richard Widmark, Kathleen Quinlan, and Robert Prosky. The film had many similarities to *Silver Streak* — both films mixed elements of comedy, romance, and suspense — as Gene once again portrayed an innocent nice guy wrongly accused of murder. In the film, Gene plays Michael Jordon (a name which now elicits laughter, though at the time the other Michael Jordan had yet to reach notoriety), a Chicago architect who has recently moved to New York. After sharing a taxi cab with a pretty young woman (Quinlan) and mailing a package for her, Michael is nearly killed by a bunch of thugs who believe he knows about a top secret computer tape. Michael tracks the young woman down at her hotel, but she just wants to be left alone. After she's shot to death, Michael finds her body and is assumed to be the murderer, leaving him no choice but to flee. Along the way he meets Kate Hellman (Radner), who believes Michael is innocent and helps him as they run from both the cops and the killers.

The film gave both Gene and Gilda ample opportunity to join together their unique brands of humor. Typical of this is one of the film's broadest scenes in which the pilot of the small plane they are flying in suddenly dies. Michael refuses to accept the fact that he now has to land the plane himself and keeps telling Kate to ask the dead pilot questions.

Upon its June 4, 1982 release, *Hanky Panky* was a failure with both audiences and critics. Years later, Gene said, "If I made one mistake professionally in my life, I think it was at that point in my life doing *Hanky Panky*. If I made one great choice in my life, it was doing *Hanky Panky* because I met Gilda, who changed where I live, how I think, how I feel, what work I do..."

When they met, Gene was living in Los Angeles while Gilda was residing in a house she had recently bought in Stamford, Connecticut. They lived together on and off for two and a half years. In 1982 they comforted each other as they each suddenly lost a close friend and colleague — on March 5, 1982, Gilda's fellow Not Ready For Prime Time Player John Belushi died of a drug overdose at age 33, and on December 2, 1982, Marty Feldman died at age 49 of a massive heart attack brought on by food poisoning on the last day of filming *Yellowbeard* (1983) in Mexico City.

In the summer of 1982, Gene took Gilda to France for a two-week holiday. Gilda had only been there once before when she was eighteen, and had found it a less than thrilling experience. With Gene as her guide, she saw France in a totally different light and, according to her, "learned it could be a pleasure and I could love it."

Shortly after they returned from France, Gene and Gilda broke up. "Gene said he was suffocating, that my needs were smothering him," Gilda wrote in her 1989 autobiography. Gilda also suffered from bulimia, something she admitted to during her *Saturday Night Live* years. But bulimia remained an ongoing struggle for Gilda, and even after she and Gene were married, she continued to force herself to vomit after dinner. It got to the point where Gene saw there was little he could do to help her and eventually just tried ignoring Gilda's eating disorder.

During their breakup, Gilda bought a dog to help her through this terribly lonely period. The female Yorkshire terrier was named Sparkle. Not long after getting Sparkle, Gene and Gilda got back together. Luckily, Gene was a dog lover (in the 1960s he adopted a small female dog named Julie) and he and Sparkle had no problem taking to one another.

For Gilda, her goal was to convince Gene to settle down and marry her. "Gene built a tennis court and a wine cellar in her Connecticut house," said Gilda's friend Pat O'Donoghue. "That made her a lot less insecure. It was sort of like an engagement ring. For a brief moment there, she was truly, finally happy." Having been married and divorced twice already, Gene was in no hurry to walk down the aisle again. In her autobiography, Gilda wrote, "My new 'career' became getting him to marry me. I turned down job offers so I could be geographically available. More often than not, I had on a white, frilly apron like Katharine Hepburn in *Woman of the Year* when she left her job to exclusively be Spencer Tracey's [sic] wife. Unfortunately, my performing ego wasn't completely content in an apron, and in every screenplay Gene was writing, or project he had under development, I finagled my way into a part."

Gilda's finagling worked, for she found herself with a part in Gene's next film, *The Woman in Red*. Victor Drai, a first-time producer who had done everything from designing clothes to selling real estate (and is now a nightclub impresario who is opening his own Vegas hotel in 2012 ), had bought the rights to a 1977 French film called *Pardon Mon Affaire*. Drai thought Gene would be ideal for the American version as a mild-mannered family man looking for a little adventure in his life. He knew Gene's agent, and soon Gene and Gilda found themselves having a series of dinners at the home of Drai and his live-in girlfriend, Kelly LeBrock.

Gene had doubts about Americanizing *Pardon Mon Affaire*. "He believed that he really didn't want to do a remake because he figured the original was so good and it's really a discredit to the original when you do one again," said cinematographer Fred Schuler. But Gene soon realized that a remake could stand on its own terms, and he ended up writing the screenplay adaptation and directing as well.

In the film, Gene plays Teddy Pierce, a shy, quiet advertising executive living in San Francisco. One day Teddy is in the parking garage of the building he works in and notices a beautiful young woman in a red dress. As she walks over a ventilation grate, her dress flies up à la Marilyn Monroe. From this moment on, Teddy becomes obsessed with pursuing this mysterious woman in red as he lies to his wife and children.

For the supporting cast, Gene assembled his old friends Charles Grodin, Joseph Bologna, and Michael Huddleston to play his male buddies who cover for him. For the title role, both Gene and Gilda thought Kelly LeBrock would be perfect. LeBrock, who was a 23-year-old model with no prior film experience, was terrified about starring in a movie, but after enough convincing, LeBrock agreed to do a screen test for Orion Pictures and soon found herself with her first film role. She found the entire experience to be very positive.

"Gene was wonderful," LeBrock said. "He was very busy but he still made time for me…The set was one of the nicest sets I've ever been on…I still hope I will find the same feeling that I had on that set. It was a family. We had a great time…There was only tension on the set one day, and that was the scene of going over the [ventilation grate]. Everyone knew it was kind of an important scene to the film, and everybody sort of got a little bit uptight. They just wanted it to be really good, and sometimes when you're on a set people get nervous off each other.

"Gene never raised his voice, he was never out of line or anything…but you could feel the tension. It was difficult because they were trying to get the dress to blow up, and it wasn't working well, and they had to change the tactic. They had to keep trying the dryers in different positions and all. And time is money on a set, and it wasn't a big budget film."

Gilda played Ms. Milner (though, as Gilda pointed out to David Letterman when promoting the film, her name is never mentioned), a hideous woman who works in Teddy's office and thinks that Teddy is really interested in her. Some critics were baffled as to why Gene would cast Gilda in such an unattractive role with not a lot of screen time. "She looks like a ghost in this movie," said Gene Siskel. "She does nothing funny." Despite such criticism, Gilda won the Best Supporting Actress award from the now defunct Your Choice for the Film Awards, an awards program whose nominees were voted on by a panel of film critics and whose winners were chosen by the public. Gilda beat out fellow nominees Peggy Ashcroft (*A Passage to India*), Christine Lahti (*Swing Shift*), Geraldine Page (*The Pope of Greenwich Village*), and Theresa Russell (*The Razor's Edge*).

To write the songs for *The Woman in Red*, Gene acquired the talents of Stevie Wonder. Wonder's songs resulted in a hugely successful soundtrack album, and his "I Just Called to Say I Love You" went on to win both an Oscar and Golden Globe for Best Original Song. In his Oscar acceptance speech, Wonder thanked Gene and dedicated the award to Nelson Mandela, who was still in prison at the time. The result was that Wonder's music was subsequently banned by the South African Broadcasting Corporation.

*The Woman in Red* opened on August 15, 1984. It was one of the first films to receive the new PG-13 rating from the MPAA, the first being *Red Dawn*, which opened a week earlier (*Dreamscape*, which opened the same day as *The Woman in Red*, also received the PG-13 rating). It did respectable business at the box office and received mixed reviews. On the positive side, Leonard Maltin called it "Wilder's best film in years," while *Time* magazine's Richard Schickel found it "a well-made sex farce of classical proportions" and "the summer's first comedy for adults." Janet Maslin of *The New York Times* wrote, "Mr. Wilder, who has improved greatly as a director, has also written the screenplay, and does it with an eye to everyone's sympathetic foibles...Whether Teddy is taking up horseback riding to impress Charlotte or turning instant hipster with a silly new suit and hairdo, Mr. Wilder manages to make him reasonably likable." Pat Collins proclaimed *The Woman in Red* the "best romantic comedy of the summer" and found Gene to be "at his irrepressible best."

A month after *The Woman in Red*'s release, Gene and Gilda were married. Gilda had been trying for the better part of two years to convince Gene to marry her, and she ended up having Sparkle to thank for Gene's proposal. "She was very insecure, terrified of so many things, afraid to be alone for the shortest period of time," Gene said. "I thought, having been married before, this could be a disaster."

Gene and Gilda were ready to leave for a vacation in France with Sparkle. They had planned to fly from Los Angeles to New York first to visit Corinne and Gil, then leave for France. While waiting in a private passenger lounge in the airport, Sparkle accidentally ate rat poison. A panicked Gilda rushed Sparkle to the vet. Gilda told Gene she would meet up with him in New York. Gilda spent the whole day at the vet's office while Gene flew to New York. When Gene landed, Gilda called him to let him know Sparkle was fine and said, "I know you love me and you know I love you. You're so tired. You need a vacation. You go on to France and when you come back I'll meet you in Connecticut and we'll be together and we'll be happy. But let's not worry about anything."

"I'd been waiting two years for her to say something like that," Gene later said. Upon his return, Gene gave Gilda an engagement ring. Orion sent them to Europe to promote *The Woman in Red*, and in between attending the Deauville Film Festival and doing interviews in Rome, Gene and Gilda found time to stop in the south of France where they were married on September 18, 1984 in the small thirteenth-century village of St. Paul-de-Vence. He was 51, she was 38. They were married by the mayor of the village in a ceremony performed in French that included only eight people, among them a Belgian couple from L.A. whom they were close friends with, some friends who owned a Danish restaurant in the south of France, Corinne and Gil, and, of course, Sparkle. The wedding party celebrated at the Danish restaurant of Gene and Gilda's friends, and later that evening Gene and Gilda enjoyed a traditional French wedding dinner in the chateau they were staying at. Since they were still in the midst of promoting *The Woman in Red*, Gene and Gilda actually spent most of their honeymoon in Rome.

When one rude French reporter asked Gene, "Why didn't you marry the beautiful girl in *The Woman in Red*?" he immediately replied, "I did!"

# 12

# Where Wolf?

While Mr. and Mrs. Wilder were adjusting to married life in Connecticut, they were already in preparation for Gene's next directorial effort, *Haunted Honeymoon*. With *The Woman in Red* having been a comfortable enough success, Orion green-lighted the picture in April 1985 with plans for a fall shoot in England. *Haunted Honeymoon* was an idea Gene had for years. He wrote the screenplay with his friend, the production designer Terence Marsh.

Set in 1930s New York, Gene and Gilda play Larry Abbot and Vickie Pearle, two successful radio actors on a program called *Manhattan Mystery Theater*. Larry and Vickie are planning to get married, but lately Larry has been experiencing nervous outbursts of hysteria on the air. It could just be pre-wedding jitters, but Larry's sponsors are furious. Larry's uncle (Paul L. Smith), a renowned psychiatrist, visits the producers and sponsors, and tells them that the way to cure Larry is to increase his sense of danger. The perfect opportunity to do this will be over the weekend as Larry and Vickie stay in the ancestral castle of Larry's eccentric Aunt Kate (Dom DeLuise in drag), where the entire Abbot family will be gathered. Unbeknownst to Larry, however, one of his greedy relatives is after his inheritance.

Filming was originally to take place in Los Angeles with some exteriors to be shot in New York, but since at the time the British pound was significantly weaker than the U.S. dollar, Orion decided it would be much more cost-efficient to shoot *Haunted Honeymoon* in England, where it could be done for nine million dollars as opposed to over thirteen million in the United States. The idea of spending a year in England was appealing to Gene, but there was one complication: England has very strict quarantine laws, and if he and Gilda wanted to bring Sparkle with them, she would have to be quarantined for six months. Gilda remained in Connecticut with Sparkle while Gene flew back and forth between England and the U.S. during the six months of pre-production and casting. For the three months Gilda was needed for actual filming, they had Sparkle cared for by Gene's secretary in California.

Shooting began in September 1985 and wrapped in mid November. Gene had tried to hold on to many of the same production crew from *The Woman in Red*. Susan Ruskin, who was an associate producer on *The Woman in Red*, was now serving as producer. Once again, Chris Greenbury was editing, John Morris was scoring, and Fred Schuler was director of photography.

"*Haunted Honeymoon* was probably the most enjoyable picture I ever worked on," Schuler said. "It was similar on *The Woman in Red*, but I felt, since we knew each other on *Haunted Honeymoon* and we had spent time beforehand discussing the script and the shoot months before in Connecticut, so when we actually did it, it felt like it was a breeze. It was a very, very pleasant experience. And we also, almost every Saturday, we went out to dinner, all of us, the whole group…and it was a real great film family."

"I think his strength is that he really can identify with the actors," Schuler continued. "He's a real actor's director. His weakness is that he hasn't done a movie [as a director] afterwards…Deep in my heart I always hope that he would do another movie and will call me, because it's such a pleasant experience…Gene is very emotional and for him making a movie is a major emotional effort. *Haunted Honeymoon* was not a very big success. And it also was Gilda's last movie, so it was a real emotional killer. And he also said, because doing two movies one after another, there's a lot of time involved to get it going and it's very exhausting, and he said he's really looking forward not to direct his next movie [but] to star in his next movie, to really do his craft."

*Haunted Honeymoon* opened on July 25, 1986 to universally bad reviews and even worse box office. In the summer of such blockbusters as *Top Gun* and *Aliens*, *Haunted Honeymoon* finished in eighth place at the box office during its opening weekend, taking in $2.7 million. One week later it was out of theaters.

"*Haunted Honeymoon* has the coherence of sweepings from a thousand cutting-room floors, the relentless mindlessness of a hamster on an exercise wheel," wrote *Newsday*'s Drew Fetherston. "Gag after dreary gag, joke after dumb joke, on it plods for much too long. It is as funny as a flogging, which it in some ways resembles."

WNBC-TV's Pia Lindstrom said, "What Gene Wilder did for *Young Frankenstein*, which this movie resembles, he does not do for *Haunted Honeymoon*...This is a send-up of the horror genre that falls flat." Lindstrom went on to say that "the jokes are few and far between," Dom DeLuise is "not given enough to do," and "Gilda Radner has no opportunity to show off her brand of humor."

*People* magazine's Ralph Novak wrote, "Connoisseurs of haunted-house comedies aren't likely to rank this among prime examples of the genre, such as Abbott & Costello's *Hold That Ghost* or Bob Hope's *Ghost Breakers*. Director Gene Wilder and his co-writer, former art director Terence Marsh, have left too many lame lines in this film about a couple who return to the man's hoary family estate to get married." Novak concluded by saying, "As writer-director of such films as *The Adventure of Sherlock Holmes' Smarter Brother*, *The World's Greatest Lover*, and *The Woman in Red*, Wilder has turned out pleasant, sporadically funny comedies. Nothing he has done, however, approaches the wild yet carefully crafted humor [Mel] Brooks generates when he gets a film rolling. Wilder almost seems too gentle, too lacking in Brooks's willingness to display an edge of nastiness. While *Haunted Honeymoon* has its entertaining moments, it makes Wilder seem almost complacent, like a ballplayer who's content to get one hit a game."

*Haunted Honeymoon* was Gene's last film as a director. Though he once said that he enjoyed directing more than acting or writing, in 2001 he looked back on his directing career with some regret. "I don't know if it was a good thing that I went into directing," he said. "I wasn't a bad director but I would never be a great director. I was trying too much to make you laugh, laugh, laugh and then put an arrow through the heart. If I'd dropped the arrow through the heart part I would have been much better off. I look at it now and say what did I go for all that schmaltz for?"

# 13

# In Sickness and in Health

The disappointment of *Haunted Honeymoon* was a blow to both Gene and Gilda, but in some ways more for Gilda. She had never really found major success in films quite the way she had on TV. *The Woman in Red* was probably her most successful role. She had been very excited about *Haunted Honeymoon*. She loved wearing the glamorous evening gowns, loved working with friends like Dom DeLuise and Julann Griffin, and, of course, was happy working with Gene. If there was any downside to her experience making the film it was that she began experiencing a series of health problems which continued even after the film came out.

Since before they got married, Gilda had tried getting pregnant, feeling it would be a surefire way to hitch Gene. After they were married, they still tried conceiving, but with no luck. It turned out Gilda's tubes were tied. Her gynecologist gave her a number of options, and Gilda ultimately decided to pursue in vitro fertilization, in which Gene's sperm would be joined in a test tube with Gilda's surgically removed eggs. Gilda was able to get pregnant but later miscarried. In February 1985, Gilda had surgery to have her tubes opened. After the procedure, Gene and Gilda needed to have sex at the exact time she was ovulating to ensure successful conception. It never happened.

Motherhood was always a dream of Gilda's, and she looked back with some regret on an illegal abortion she had when she was nineteen that she felt "probably influenced the messy state of my reproductive organs."

While they were in England filming *Haunted Honeymoon*, Gilda found out she was pregnant. She and Gene were ecstatic but only let a select few know. The happiness was not long lasting, however, for Gilda had a miscarriage a week later. Gene and Gilda dealt with the miscarriage privately but decided now maybe wasn't the best time for Gilda to get pregnant considering the demands of making a movie, so they started using birth control and decided to put off trying to conceive until they returned back to the States.

About a week after the miscarriage, Gilda began developing flu-like symptoms. The studio was always cold and damp, so she didn't think anything unusual was happening, but she no longer had the intense energy she used to. She simply did not feel well.

After filming was completed, Gene and Gilda returned to the United States. Gilda was thrilled to be reunited with Sparkle and was able to muster up enough energy to prepare Thanksgiving dinner. In January 1986, as they were driving to a friend's house in Los Angeles to play tennis, Gilda felt what she described as a "fog rolling in." She was overcome with an extreme sense of tiredness and found it difficult to keep her eyes open. This lasted about forty-five minutes and then she was fine, but the listlessness continued. Now she was worried. The next day, she went to see her internist, who gave her a complete physical and informed her she had Epstein-Barr virus. The doctor said it was not life-threatening and would go away.

The tiredness continued on and off, however. Gilda would be fine for days at a time and then suddenly not have enough energy to get out of bed. Gilda became very depressed and again went to see her doctor, who suspected what Gilda had was psychological, a result of her miscarriage six months earlier. Gilda's health problems continued, but no doctor could find anything wrong.

In June she and Gene went to the south of France for a holiday. She still wasn't feeling like her old self, but the fatigue wasn't quite as bad as it had been and for the first time in months Gilda was enjoying herself. On their last night in France, they flew to Paris, and as they were walking towards the rue de Rivoli to find a taxi, Gilda experienced severe stomach pains. They returned to Connecticut, and Gilda continued seeing doctors, each one telling her nothing was wrong. She even went to see a doctor in Boston who specialized in Epstein-Barr virus. He told her that her symptoms fit that of Epstein-Barr and she should just continue to get regular blood work done. When the doctor asked her what she was so afraid of, Gilda said, "I'm afraid I have cancer." The doctor assured her what she had was not life-threatening.

For Gilda, cancer was something she always feared. A brain tumor is what claimed her beloved father when Gilda was fourteen, and in the early '70s her mother had a mastectomy after a bout with breast cancer. According to Gene, Gilda "made jokes about cancer almost every day of her life, I think in the hope that if she joked about it and said it out loud often enough, God would say, 'Well, I certainly can't give it to her *now!*'" (In her 1980 Broadway performance film *Gilda Live*, Gilda, as Long Island Jewish singer Rhonda Weiss, tells the audience about her fear that the FDA will ban saccharin from the market, saying, "I'm sorry about the lab animals, but statistics prove that most guys prefer skinny girls with cancer over healthy girls with bulging thighs.")

In July, Gene and Gilda did publicity for *Haunted Honeymoon*. After the film opened and shortly thereafter closed, Gilda began experiencing other symptoms: she became very bloated, her clothes felt tight, and she was having a lot of gas. She went to an acupuncturist, a holistic doctor, and even a new gynecologist, but still no one could find anything and Gilda's frustration only grew. Gene was offered a movie called *Grandfather* that was to begin filming in Paris in November. Gilda told Gene she didn't feel up to going with him and wanted to stay home and concentrate on writing.

On October 20, 1986, Gilda received a phone call from her internist. He told her that one of the tests he performed on her showed an irregularity in her liver function. Three days later, the internist checked Gilda into Century City Hospital for tests. She had a CAT scan and fluid was drawn from her abdomen. The following day, on October 24, 1986, Gilda was given the news she had feared: she had stage IV ovarian cancer, the most lethal of all pelvic cancers. She and Gene were devastated. On October 26th, surgery was performed to remove a grapefruit sized tumor. The surgery also included a complete hysterectomy, dashing Gilda's dream of ever having a child of her own. Gene backed out of doing *Grandfather* (the film wound up never being made) and remained by Gilda's side the entire time. After the surgery, Gilda developed pneumonia and had a fever of 104. She remained in intensive care for five days.

The tabloids were eager to find out what was going on with Gilda, and they eventually discovered the pseudonym under which Gilda was registered at the hospital: Lily Herman (Herman for her father and Lily because it was what she wanted to name her baby if it was a girl). The hospital then had Gene and Gilda's names changed to Lorna and Stanley Blake. The *National Enquirer* ran a story titled "Gilda Radner Cancer Tragedy — The Heartbreaking Untold Story." It was filled with the usual array of quotes from various "inside sources." In response, Gene issued a press release simply stating that Gilda was diagnosed with ovarian cancer, had surgery, and a full recovery was expected.

During her hospital stay, Gene would go shopping in Beverly Hills and shower Gilda with gifts (he even managed to sneak Sparkle in without any hospital staff finding out). Gilda was released from the hospital three weeks after her surgery and had to begin a series of nine chemotherapy treatments, one every three weeks. What lay ahead would be the most difficult and painful ordeal Gilda would ever have to endure, and for Gene, he would have to give the bravest performance of his life.

# 14

# Road to Wellness

By the time Gilda returned home from the hospital she was frail and weighed only ninety-five pounds. Her ensuing medical treatment was aggressive. In addition to nine months of chemotherapy, which left her bald, Gilda endured thirty radiation treatments, as well as four intraperitoneal washes, in which anti-tumor drugs were infused directly into her abdomen. Gilda was scared. She often would wake up in the middle of the night, sweaty and out of breath, and cry as Gene would hold her and tell her that everything was going to be all right.

In addition to Gene, Gilda had a strong support system in her girlfriends Pam Katz and Judy Levy (sister-in-law of Eugene Levy), her friend Grace Ayrsman, who was the caretaker of Gene and Gilda's Connecticut house, and a nurse from the hospital named Jodi, who continued to care for Gilda at home. But it was a psychotherapist named Joanna Bull who helped Gilda take a more active role in her cancer treatment at a time when she felt totally helpless. Bull visited Gilda during her second week in the hospital and, according to Gilda, "it was as though an angel had walked into my hospital room." As executive director of The Wellness Community, a cancer self-help group in Santa Monica, Bull specialized in counseling cancer patients and had successfully fought leukemia herself.

Bull thought Gilda would benefit from going to The Wellness Community, which was non-profit, free of charge, and designed to help cancer patients get a handle on their illness by talking to others with the disease. In January 1987, Gilda attended her first group therapy session at The Wellness Community. She was hesitant about going. "The last place I thought I wanted to go was somewhere where everyone else was sick too," she said. But she found The Wellness Community — with its special events such as Joke Fests and potluck dinners — to be just what she needed. "It's not voo-doo [sic]," Gilda said. "It's just a bunch of comrades-in-arms united against a common enemy. I've come to realize that with all the great medical care I was receiving, and all the support from my family and friends, there was still something missing: *None of those people had cancer.*"

By December 1987, Gilda had finished the last of her radiation treatments and her cancer was now in remission. As Gilda's strength started to return, she and Gene looked forward to 1988 being a banner year. *Life* magazine did a cover story on her for their March 1988 issue titled "Gilda Radner's Answer to Cancer: Healing the Body With Mind and Heart." The article dealt with Gilda's cancer battle, her remission, and the comfort she found in The Wellness Community.

In addition to the *Life* article, both Gene and Gilda were getting back to work. Gene was one of many Actors Studio alums who appeared in *Hello Actors Studio*, a three-hour documentary that was briefly shown in art houses in 1988 and has rarely been seen since. He was also working on the screenplay for *See No Evil, Hear No Evil*, which he would shortly begin filming with Richard Pryor, while Gilda was making a return to television in a guest spot on the Showtime cable series *It's Garry Shandling's Show*, which her good friend Alan Zweibel produced. Gilda played herself, stopping by Shandling's house to drop off videotapes he had lent her to cheer her up when she was sick. Gene was affectionately acknowledged when the end credits appear over the portrait of him as Dr. Frankenstein's grandfather from *Young Frankenstein.*

Before going on to do the Shandling show, Gilda was terribly insecure and actually worried that the audience wouldn't remember who she was. But as soon as Gilda appeared, the audience went wild. Gilda ate it up. When Shandling tells her not to milk the applause, she explains it's been a while since she appeared on television. He asks her what was wrong and she says, "Oh, I had cancer. What'd you have?"

Knowing she could still make people laugh made Gilda ecstatic. Gilda's appearance on Shandling's show was such a success that it earned her an Emmy nomination for Outstanding Guest Performer in a Comedy Series and several offers to do her own sitcom.

Three days after taping the Shandling show, Gilda had to be admitted to the hospital for complications resulting from her radiation treatment. She remained in the hospital for eight days, but the upside was that at least it was not because the cancer had returned. Gilda was still not out of the woods, though. As the *Life* article had clearly pointed out, the survival rate for ovarian cancer was then just thirty percent (it has since risen to forty-five percent) and Gilda wouldn't be considered in the clear unless her remission continued for a year and a half.

During this period, Gilda devoted three hours a day to writing a book about her experience with cancer, appropriately titled *It's Always Something*, Roseanne Roseannadanna's favorite truism on life. In one of the book's final passages, Gilda wrote, "I had wanted to wrap this book up in a neat little package about a girl who is a comedienne from Detroit, becomes famous in New York, with all the world coming her way, gets this horrible disease of cancer, is brave and fights it, learning all the skills she needs to get through it, and then, miraculously, things are neatly tied up and she gets well. I wanted to be able to write on the book jacket 'Her triumph over cancer' or 'She wins the cancer war.' I wanted a perfect ending, so I sat down to write a book with the ending in place before there even *was* an ending. Now I've learned, the hard way, that some poems don't rhyme, and some stories don't have a clear beginning, middle and end. Like my life, this book has ambiguity. Like my life, this book is about not knowing, having to change, taking the moment and making the best of it, without knowing what's going to happen next."

# 15

# Color Blind
# Movie Magic

It had been nine years since Gene Wilder and Richard Pryor had last worked together. Fans of *Silver Streak* and *Stir Crazy* had long hoped America's favorite salt and pepper comedy team would reunite. In 1989 those fans got their wish when Wilder and Pryor starred in *See No Evil, Hear No Evil*, which again gave them the opportunity to work with Arthur Hiller, who directed them in *Silver Streak*. Why did it take almost a decade for Wilder and Pryor to get back together on-screen? According to Gene, "I know it's hard to believe, but nobody asked."

Actually, both Wilder and Pryor had been attached to the 1983 comedy *Trading Places*. Pryor dropped out, however, to do *The Toy* (1982) with Jackie Gleason. Eddie Murphy, who was cast in Pryor's place, didn't want to work with Gene because, according to Murphy biographer Frank Sanello, "he feared being too closely identified with Pryor's screen persona." Murphy had helped Paramount Pictures score a major hit with *48HRS.* (1982), so when he lobbied to get Gene replaced with Dan Aykroyd, the studio acquiesced.

Producer Marvin Worth had been developing the script for *See No Evil, Hear No Evil* for years. The first draft was written by Earl Barrett and Arne Sultan, perhaps best known for producing the Ted Knight sitcom *Too Close for Comfort*. Hiller had actually been sent an early draft of the script years before Wilder and Pryor were involved with the project, and wasn't interested in it at the time, feeling it "lacked something." Worth brought the *Saturday Night Live* writing team of Eliot Wald and Andrew Kurtzman in to do a rewrite. Hiller liked the new script, but Worth and Tri-Star were interested in casting a pair of younger actors in the lead roles. Hiller talked the studio into considering Wilder and Pryor.

Both Wilder and Pryor felt the script had problems. "It didn't ring true, and the characters weren't defined," Gene said. Gene convinced the studio to let him rewrite the first twenty-two pages of the script. He told Tri-Star that if they didn't like his reworking of the script, "No hard feelings. Don't pay me a thing." But the studio did like Gene's rewrite and gave the film the go-ahead.

Hiller was impressed with the generosity Gene demonstrated in his rewrite. "I said, boy, he's writing, he's the star, he could take all the good things [for himself]," Hiller said. "[But] he wrote so many wonderful scenes for Richard Pryor. There's no ego in acting terms at all."

In *See No Evil, Hear No Evil*, Pryor plays Wally, a blind man who refuses to accept his disability and tries to cover up by reading newspapers (upside down) on the subway and looking through binoculars (in the wrong direction) at the racetrack. Wilder plays Dave, a deaf man who, after losing his hearing eight years ago, has given up his acting career and now operates a newsstand in Manhattan's Union Square.

One day Wally goes to Dave's newsstand for a job, and after some very funny mishaps, Dave hires Wally. A little time passes, and then one day Wally's bookie visits the newsstand and, as Dave's back is turned, is murdered. Dave couldn't hear the gunshots, but he did catch a glimpse of the killer's sultry legs. Wally couldn't see anything but he did smell her perfume. Now the police suspect Wally and Dave are the killers, but after escaping from the police station, Wally uses his hearing and Dave uses his sight to go in search of the real killers (Joan Severance and a pre-Oscar-winning Kevin Spacey).

Taking what was familiar territory for Wilder and Pryor — nice guys accused of a crime they didn't commit — and adding the blind and deaf angle made *See No Evil, Hear No Evil* an acting challenge for both leads. They were very concerned about offending blind and deaf people, so Wilder and Pryor studied at the New York League for the Hard of Hearing and the Braille Institute in California, respectively. "I wanted to make sure the deafness and the blindness was taken for real," Gene told Joel Siegel. "Even though it's a comedy — all the more reason why it had to be based in reality."

Despite Wilder and Pryor's attention to detail and their attempts not to make a mockery out of people with disabilities, there were some in Hollywood's deaf community who were less than amused with the film. "They use our disability to make gags, to make fun of it, and that really encourages the stereotype of who we are," said Phyllis Frelich, the deaf actress who originated the role of Sarah Norman in the Broadway production of *Children of a Lesser God* (the role Marlee Matlin later played on film). It was exactly this kind of unwarranted controversy Gene was looking to avoid when writing the film and preparing for his role. "We wanted to make sure — Richard and I — that we weren't going to offend anyone," Gene said, "but on the contrary that they would be happy that we were doing it because it would increase the awareness of what it's like."

Thankfully, it was only a very select few who seemed to have a problem with *See No Evil, Hear No Evil*. The New York League for the Hard of Hearing agreed with Gene's defense of the film. "There were communication tips woven through the film," said the League's Ruth Green, "but basically the film is a comedy. And it's fun. And you laugh."

The sign language expert Gene studied with was a 46-year-old divorcee named Karen Webb. "So I said, well, I think [it would be] a good idea if he could come in and experience some of the speech reading classes and meet some people so that he could portray that person as honestly as he could…" Webb said. "And I found him delightful and charming. He showed very much respect to all of our clients and to the people he met. And, of course, they were very excited to meet him."

Having not worked together for almost a decade, many — including Wilder and Pryor themselves — pondered whether the chemistry they previously had would still exist after such a long hiatus. "You wonder after eight years," Gene said, "will it be nervous time? Will you get along and all that. It was easier. It was like a knife going through soft butter. It was like coming home again. I've never had that experience with another actor. It was very comforting to know whatever it is between us is still there."

In the nine years between *Stir Crazy* and *See No Evil, Hear No Evil*, both Wilder and Pryor had been through a lot in their personal lives. For Gene, of course, there was Gilda's cancer ordeal. As for Pryor, he nearly died in 1980 when he caught fire while freebasing cocaine. He also went through his fifth divorce and began having health problems that led to rumors he had AIDS (he was later diagnosed with multiple sclerosis). Both men felt these experiences made them much mellower than they were while doing *Stir Crazy*.

During publicity for *See No Evil, Hear No Evil*, virtually every interviewer asked both Wilder and Pryor what the secret of their rapport is. They even asked each other. "We don't know the answer to it," Pryor said. "You just be grateful that it happens to you… Something happened with us. And it's nice."

Gene tried analyzing their on-screen connection in a more interesting way. "We have almost a sexual relationship," Gene said. "It's like lovers. When we see each other on the set there's a certain nervousness, a little anticipation. We're very spontaneous. I could say anything during a take, even if he never saw it before [and] he would respond, just as if it was written in the script, and vice versa. And there's an energy that's there that people call a chemistry, but I call it an energy, like a sexual energy. And when we finish filming for the day, we go home. We don't talk to each other and we don't see each other socially. And I'm telling you it's almost as if [we're] lovers who have just met — they're afraid to spoil it for the next time."

Arthur Hiller summed up the Wilder-Pryor magic very simply. "They are both actors with good comedy sense," Hiller said. "It wasn't like putting two comedians together. They work very well with each other and off each other."

Despite the outward happiness Pryor displayed during interviews for *See No Evil, Hear No Evil*, he did not think much of it, calling the finished film "lackluster." Having recently been diagnosed with multiple sclerosis, he started to feel the toll of the disease during filming. Pryor admitted his motivation for doing *See No Evil, Hear No Evil* was not to reunite with Gene so much as it was for financial reasons. "My excuse was the money," Pryor wrote in his autobiography. "I don't know what everybody else had in mind. Physically and emotionally, it was difficult to involve myself in the work." *

*See No Evil, Hear No Evil* opened on May 12, 1989. Critical praise was mixed. Vincent Canby of *The New York Times* called it "the first pop comedy of the year that is really funny" and wrote that "Wilder and Pryor have never worked better together." Kevin Thomas of the *Los Angeles Times* called it "brisk, ingenious and funny," while the *Today* show's Gene Shalit declared it "the funniest movie of the year so far."

Among the critics who spoke evil of Gene Wilder and Richard Pryor's third film together was Roger Ebert, who noted that the film had "a fatal problem: Both of its heroes are nice guys. Wilder and Pryor both play loving, sensitive, kind and gentle souls, and that would be wonderful in life, but a movie needs some edge to it. I doubt if Gene Wilder has it in him to play a mean-spirited, vindictive character, but Pryor use to be able to call on that other side. He became a movie star by being a wise guy. In recent years, however, he seems to have locked himself into a series of sweet roles in which the cutting edge of his personality remains concealed." Rex Reed, never known for mincing words, called the film "a nightmare" and "a trough of swill," adding that "there isn't one shred of humor, originality or intelligence in the entire film."

*See No Evil, Hear No Evil* was the number one film at the box office for two weeks straight and took in more than $46 million. It wasn't as big a moneymaker as the two previous Wilder-Pryor pairings, but it was a hit nonetheless. Unfortunately, Gene was not able to enjoy the film's success. At the same time he was on top at the box office, he would also lose Gilda.

---

* Pryor's disappointment with *See No Evil, Hear No Evil* echoes how he felt about his first film with Gene. Despite the huge success of *Silver Streak*, Pryor told Janet Maslin in an August 1977 interview for *The New York Times*, "I put myself in it, but I didn't *do* it, not with my heart. It was a business decision. I was looking to hustle, and I got hustled."

# 16

# The Day
# the Laughter Died

When Gilda was diagnosed with cancer, Gene stopped working completely to be with her. In early 1988, when she was in remission, Gene got involved with *See No Evil, Hear No Evil*, feeling that Gilda was on the road back to total health. But by May of 1988, Gilda was given the news that the cancer had returned. Gilda's plans for her own sitcom were put on hold, but Gene was already committed to *See No Evil, Hear No Evil*.

"Gilda was so sick, some days I wondered how he could work," recalled Arthur Hiller. "He was worried so much about her...He talked about it but he didn't make a 'thing' out of it. But I certainly was aware how ill she was."

After Gilda's recurrence, she had to have more chemotherapy and in October 1988 underwent surgery to repair an obstructed bowel. She even changed her eating habits dramatically, going on a strict macrobiotic diet in the hopes it would contribute to healing her body.

By early 1989, Gilda finished her book, and Simon and Schuster planned to publish it in the summer. Gilda made her last public appearance in January 1989 with Gene at a benefit for The Wellness Community and looked radiant, better than she had since her illness first struck. But the following months would see Gilda's health decline steadily. "I was so incredibly dumb," Gene said. "I thought she was going to pull through up until three weeks before she died…I could see that she wasn't going to make it. And she knew it too." She never gave up fighting, though — on April 3, 1989, she went into a recording studio to read *It's Always Something* for the book-on-audio version. "She'd pull herself out of bed," Gene remembers, "put a little makeup on, put a skirt and blouse on, be driven to the studio, record her book, come home, and get back into bed."

Meanwhile Gene was doing publicity for *See No Evil, Hear No Evil*. When he appeared on *Later with Bob Costas*, Costas asked Gene how Gilda was doing. "Great," he replied. "She is. As you know, she's been through rough times, but she's doing great now. She's doing so well that she's out promoting her book…"

But Gilda was not doing well and was not out promoting her book. At the *See No Evil, Hear No Evil* premiere on May 7, 1989, Gene showed up alone. Gilda was dying. "Oh, God, my mind is 100 percent but my body is like a 4," Gilda told a Toronto friend, Janet Siskind Robertson, in March 1989.

On Wednesday, May 17, 1989, Gilda checked into Cedars-Sinai Medical Center in Los Angeles. She was going to have a CAT scan performed but, according to Gene, "the people there couldn't keep her on the gurney. She was raving like a crazed woman — she knew they would give her morphine and she was afraid she'd never regain consciousness." Gilda was sedated and remained unconscious for three days. Gene was by her side the entire time until a doctor finally told him to go home and get some sleep. At 4:00 a.m. on Saturday, May 20th, there was a knock on Gene's door. It was an old friend, a surgeon, who told Gene, "Come on. It's time to go." When Gene arrived at the hospital, a night nurse had washed Gilda and removed all of her tubes. "She looked like an angel," Gene recalled. "So peaceful. She was still alive, and as she lay there, I kissed her." Gilda's breathing had become irregular. Two hours after Gene arrived, Gilda died in her sleep at 6:20 a.m. She was six weeks shy of her forty-third birthday. "While she was conscious," Gene said, "I never said good-bye."

News of Gilda's death came as a shock to the entertainment community and indeed the world, as many had believed Gilda really was doing well. The Saturday that she died, Steve Martin was hosting *Saturday Night Live*. Martin, who had worked with Gilda numerous times on the show, as well as in the 1985 movie *Movers & Shakers*, paid tribute to Gilda and showed the classic "Dancing in the Dark" sketch they had done in 1978.

Gilda was laid to rest on May 24, 1989 near her Connecticut home at Long Ridge Union Cemetery, the same nondenominational cemetery where jazz great Benny Goodman and boxer Gene Tunney are buried. "It was a beautiful ceremony, small," said Gene and Gilda's Stamford neighbor Howard Orlo. "It was pouring and thundering," continued Howard's wife Elaine. "I remember they had a tent, it was outside and the rain [was] just dripping down and [it was thundering]…I think Gene or one of her friends said, 'There's Gilda. She's here. She's listening. She's taking it in.'"

Considering how protective he is of his personal life, it was only natural that Gene would grieve for Gilda privately. He made occasional public appearances in the months following Gilda's death, such as one at a benefit luncheon for the New York League for the Hard of Hearing with Karen Webb, who had now become a close friend. But it wasn't until a year after Gilda's death that Gene actually talked about his loss and Gilda's ultimately losing fight against cancer. In the spring of 1990 Gene appeared on the first edition of a new CBS program called *Face to Face with Connie Chung*. In a very candid interview, Gene admitted what helped him put on a brave front for Gilda during her illness: "I only had one great thing going for me: I thought she was going to pull it out," he said. "I never thought she would die. Never. And sometimes she would grab my hand and look at me, stare right into my soul and say, 'Really? Really?' And I'd say, 'If I could live as long as you're going to live I'd settle right now.' And I meant it. I thought that I would die before she did. I thought she would make it."

There was another reason Gene was talking. Shortly after Gilda died, Gene read an article in *The New York Times* entitled "Research Links Diet and Infertility Factors to Ovarian Cancer." Gene sent a letter to Larry Altman, who wrote the article, and asked him a number of key questions about ovarian cancer. Altman suggested that Gene might want to talk with Dr. M. Steven Piver, who

specialized in treating ovarian cancer at the Roswell Park Cancer
Institute in Buffalo, New York. Gene called Dr. Piver and it was a
phone call that ultimately turned into a unique friendship and partnership. Not wanting Gilda's death to be in vain, the two decided
to join forces and start a campaign to let women know about the
risks of ovarian cancer.

Early diagnosis is the key to successfully treating ovarian cancer.
Because the ovaries are located deep within the pelvis, it is difficult to detect any abnormalities. It is now believed that family
history is a key factor in determining a woman's risk for getting
ovarian cancer. Gilda knew that her first cousin, Lenore Goodman Rosa, had successfully fought ovarian cancer. Gilda's maternal
aunt, Elsie Rhineston, died of ovarian cancer, and Gilda's maternal
grandmother, Goldie Dworkin, who was believed to have died of
stomach cancer, likely had ovarian cancer, which years ago was
often diagnosed as stomach cancer. Add to that the fact that Gilda's
mother had breast cancer and, according to Dr. Piver, Gilda had an
almost 50-50 chance of developing cancer herself. But Gilda was
unaware of the hereditary link.

In 1990 Gene appeared in a public service announcement titled
"Please Don't Be Afraid, Just Do It," written by Dr. Piver, in which
he urged women at risk for ovarian cancer to see their doctor and
get a pelvic exam, a sonogram, and a blood test called CA125, three
tools now believed to help in the detection of ovarian cancer. But,
as Gene and Dr. Piver had stressed, early detection is the key. "If
she had been diagnosed nine, eight, seven, six months before, I'm
not telling you that I know, but I would bet my bottom dollar that
she'd be alive today," Gene told Connie Chung.

"People write to me," Gene said, "and call it Gilda's disease. People
weren't talking about ovarian cancer. But Gilda Radner died of
what? Ovarian cancer. So now people want to know about it, happily so. I just wish Gilda had been one of the people who had read
about Gilda's disease and could have benefited from it."

On May 9, 1991, Gene appeared before a House subcommittee
to talk about how women need to know the facts about ovarian
cancer. "At first I didn't think it would make a difference if I testi-
fied, but we have to learn from the past," he told *People* magazine

in a cover story they did entitled "Gilda Didn't Have to Die." In 1996, Gene collaborated with Dr. Piver on *Gilda's Disease*, a detailed, straightforward book about ovarian cancer that combined important medical information with personal insight from Gene and Joanna Bull, as well as excerpts of letters Gene had received from fans and women with ovarian cancer.

When Connie Chung asked Gene if the grieving process was over, he replied, "A certain part is over and I'm concentrating on being as happy and doing as many meaningful things as I can do, so to that extent the grieving is over. There's another part that doesn't ever end. I don't want it to end. It keeps me on my toes. [After] all the chemotherapies, all the pain and the torture, the truth is it was fun. It was fun. It was the best years of my life. Truly."

# 17

# Back to Work

It was the fall of 1989. Gilda had been dead about five months. Gene was vacationing in Amsterdam when he got a message to call his agent in California about a wonderful script that had come along unlike anything he had ever done. He called his agent, who told him the script was a comedy, it was going to be released by Paramount, and Leonard Nimoy would be directing. Having not worked for a while and still emotionally fragile, Gene had doubts about doing another movie so soon after Gilda's death, but the script, then called *New York Times*, really moved him.

"I read it and I thought, Why me?" Gene said. "I know why me, but how did they know that this is right for me? Because it's different from anything I've done. It's a beautiful love story. Serious but funny."

The script was based on an *Esquire* article by Bob Greene entitled "Convention of the Love Goddesses" that Paramount had bought the rights to. Norman Steinberg and David Frankel wrote the screenplay, which was retitled *Funny About Love*. The film particularly touched a nerve with Gene because of its dealing with a couple having difficulty conceiving a child, as he and Gilda did.

Gene plays Duffy Bergman, a popular political cartoonist à la Garry Trudeau. The film opens at a book signing where Duffy, a connoisseur of coffee, tastes the worst cup of cappuccino he's ever had. He insists on meeting who made this dreadful coffee. She turns out to be Meg Lloyd (Christine Lahti), an attractive young caterer. Duffy immediately changes his tune about the coffee and after the book signing asks Meg out.

The two eventually move in together and then marry but there's one thing missing: a child. When Meg has trouble getting pregnant, she endures numerous medical procedures, such as in vitro fertilization, with no success. The medical scenes are actually among the funniest in the film, especially when Duffy is the one going through tests. In one scene, the doctor presents Duffy with a special pair of underwear to lower the temperature of his sperm. "What's this little pocket for?" asks Duffy. "Ice," responds the doctor. The next scene has Duffy painfully trying to walk down the street with ice in his pants as Meg attempts helping him.

The strain of wanting to have a baby leads Duffy and Meg to break up. During their separation, Duffy meets Daphne DeLillo (Mary Stuart Masterson), a very young, tough-talking TV sports producer who he begins a romance with. Farrah Fawcett was in the film as Duffy's college girlfriend, but Nimoy disliked her personally and hated her performance, resulting in him completely cutting her from the finished film.

*Funny About Love* was different for Gene in that his character was very serious at times, and there are two scenes where Duffy actually cries (one after the death of his mother, the other when Meg moves out). According to Christine Lahti, "He was pretty raw. But what surprised me about Gene — I knew he was a funny man, I knew he had just gone through, of course, all this horrible stuff — but I didn't know how great an actor he was. He was able to use a lot of that pain through this piece and in this character, and that's not easy to do. It must have been hard for him…"

When asked if going back to work after Gilda's death was indeed hard, Gene told *Good Morning America*'s Charles Gibson that it was actually easy. "I don't think I was expressing my feelings fully for a long time," he said. "And I'm an actor since thirteen years old. When I got on the set with people who were very sympathetic, very friendly — we didn't talk about any of these things — but when the scenes came up, very loving scenes and then separation, things came out of me during the day on the set that weren't coming out of me during the day in life. And when I got home at night, instead of feeling worse I felt better...It was good therapy for me."

*Funny About Love* opened on September 21, 1990. The critical response was anything but funny. Roger Ebert wrote, "The new movie *Funny About Love* provides an opportunity to spend 101 minutes in the presence of the most cloying, inane, and annoying dialogue I've heard in many a moon, punctuated by occasional lapses into startling bad manners." *Newsday*'s Terry Kelleher concurred, calling the film "extremely annoying." Janet Maslin of *The New York Times* wasn't quite as harsh, noting that Wilder and Lahti were both "miraculously likable under difficult circumstances."

The *New York Post*'s Jami Bernard gave the film a mixed review, but wrote, "The refreshing thing about this movie is that everyone has a distinct sense of humor, even the couple's pediatrician. Some clearly improvised moments catch the cast members off guard." Bernard seemed somewhat uncomfortable with Gene's real-life connection to the film. "Then there is the Gilda Radner thing," she wrote. "It would be nice if we could take a movie out of the context of what has happened to its actors, but everyone knows that Wilder only recently lost the wife on whom he doted. He has put his heart and soul into this surprisingly dramatic part, resulting in scenes where his pain looks heartrendingly real. Nimoy cuts away from that pain out of a sense of intrusion on an actor's grief. No amount of comedy will compensate." Joel Siegel was kindest in his review. "Wilder is just one of the best comic actors around," he said. He also had praise for Lahti, but was troubled by how the film dealt with fertility problems. "You can do a comedy about people who want a baby and have a baby," Siegel said, "but wanting a baby and not having one is too tragic. That's not funny. That's why *Funny About Love* isn't."

*Funny About Love* finished in fifth place at the box office during its opening weekend, taking in a total of $3 million dollars. It quickly dropped after that and was out of theaters by its third week, taking in a domestic total of $8 million dollars.

According to Norman Steinberg, Nimoy made so many changes to the original script that by the time filming was completed it was quite literally a different movie. "I was bitterly disappointed," Steinberg said. "I wish it hadn't been made. It was such a good script. I could probably take the [first draft of the] script out and sell it as a totally different film."

Greene's article was about a guy who couldn't get a date in college but is now a big success and returns to give a speech to a sorority convention at his alma mater. In the audience are three women who have had key roles in his life, and, in the first draft of the screenplay, the film flashed back and forth in time as he reflects on his relationships with them. Originally, Duffy was written as a much younger man, in his late thirties or so (Gene was 56 when he did the movie). In one draft of the script, instead of being a cartoonist, Duffy was a stand-up comic. That version of the script was sent to Robin Williams, who passed on it.

Despite the film's failure, Gene found making it a positive experience. He found Nimoy to be a very sensitive director, and, being that he was also an actor, was able to have a sort of shorthand with him (the two have remained friends through the years). As for Lahti, Gene instantly connected with her and said she is "maybe the best actress I've ever worked with."

During filming, Gene told one interviewer, "In my opinion, this is the best film I've done since *Young Frankenstein*." Several years later, he mused, "I should've been funnier in that film, no?"

Gene Wilder, then Jerome Silberman, in his 1951 high school graduation picture.

Jerome Silberman, several years before becoming Gene Wilder, in his 1955 graduation photo from the University of Iowa.

Gene Wilder's birth certificate.

Sal Mineo, Michael Tolan, Peter Falk, Gene Wilder, and Robert Lansing in the 1962 *DuPont Show of the Week* production "A Sound of Hunting." Gene was 28 years old. This was one of his first television roles and the earliest known photo of him acting on-screen. © 1962 National Broadcasting Company, Inc.

A 34-year-old Gene Wilder in a publicity shot for *The Producers.* © 1968 Embassy Pictures.

It's a Nazi party! Zero Mostel, Kenneth Mars, and Gene Wilder in *The Producers.*
© 1968 Embassy Pictures.

A man and his little blue blanket. The role of Leo Bloom in *The Producers* earned Gene Wilder an Academy Award nomination for Best Supporting Actor and helped make him a star. © 1968 Embassy Pictures.

Wigging out. Donald Sutherland and Gene Wilder in *Start the Revolution Without Me*. © 1970 Warner Bros. Inc.

Who could resist that *Yiddishe punim?* Gene Wilder as the peasant Claude in *Start the Revolution Without Me.* © 1970 Warner Bros. Inc.

The candy man can! Peter Ostrum, Gene Wilder, and Jack Albertson in *Willy Wonka & the Chocolate Factory.* © 1971 Warner Bros. Inc.

Wilder and wooly. Dr. Doug Ross (Gene Wilder) finds true love with a sheep named Daisy in *Everything You Always Wanted to Know About Sex But Were Afraid to Ask*. © 1972 United Artists Corporation.

Don't tell Mel! Gene Wilder and Anne Bancroft in the 1974 ABC variety special *Annie and the Hoods*. © 1974 American Broadcasting Companies, Inc.

"I just called to say I love you." Gene Wilder as Harry Evers in *Thursday's Game.* © 1974 American Broadcasting Companies, Inc.

Crazy like a fox. Steven Warner tries taming Gene Wilder in *The Little Prince.* © 1974 Stanley Donen Films Inc. and Paramount Pictures Corporation.

Gene Wilder as the boozy gunslinger Jim (a.k.a. the Waco Kid) in *Blazing Saddles.*
© 1974 Warner Bros. Inc.

Gene called making *Young Frankenstein* "the happiest film experience I've ever had." From the loving smile on Mel Brooks' face, the joy was contagious as Brooks watches Teri Garr, Peter Boyle, Gene, and Marty Feldman rehearse on the set. © 1974 Twentieth Century-Fox Film Corporation.

Teri Garr, Gene Wilder, Madeline Kahn, and Marty Feldman are some of the actors who made up what Gene called "the best comedy cast ever assembled" in *Young Frankenstein.* © 1974 Twentieth Century-Fox Film Corporation.

Gene Wilder romances Madeline Kahn in *The Adventure of Sherlock Holmes' Smarter Brother*. © 1975 Twentieth Century-Fox Film Corporation.

Gene Wilder gives Marty Feldman some direction on the set of *The Adventure of Sherlock Holmes' Smarter Brother*. © 1975 Twentieth Century-Fox Film Corporation.

All aboard! Scatman Crothers, Richard Pryor, Gene Wilder, and Jill Clayburgh in a publicity still for *Silver Streak*. © 1976 Twentieth Century-Fox Film Corporation.

Gene Wilder and Richard Pryor teamed up for the first of four films in *Silver Streak*. © 1976 Twentieth Century-Fox Film Corporation.

A Jewish Valentino? Gene Wilder as Rudy Valentine in *The World's Greatest Lover*. © 1977 Twentieth Century-Fox Film Corporation.

Carol Kane, Gene Wilder, and Gene's real-life cousin Mark "Buddy" Silberman in *The World's Greatest Lover*. © 1977 Twentieth Century-Fox Film Corporation.

Hi-*oy*, Silver! Gene Wilder as Rabbi Avram Belinski in *The Frisco Kid*.
© 1979 Warner Bros. Inc.

Harrison Ford and Gene Wilder rest their *tucheses* on the set of *The Frisco Kid*.
© 1979 Warner Bros. Inc.

Sidney Poitier and Gene Wilder have a reflective moment on the set of *Stir Crazy*. © 1980 Columbia Pictures Industries, Inc.

Life behind bars makes Harry Monroe (Richard Pryor) and Skip Donahue (Gene Wilder) go *Stir Crazy*. © 1980 Columbia Pictures Industries, Inc.

Gene and Gilda share a laugh during a break from filming *Hanky Panky* in the summer of 1981. © 1982 Columbia Pictures Industries, Inc.

Teddy Pierce (Gene Wilder) pursues the beautiful Charlotte (Kelly LeBrock) in *The Woman in Red.* © 1984 Orion Pictures Corporation.

Larry Abbot (Gene Wilder) and Vickie Pearle (Gilda Radner) are 1930s
radio actors in *Haunted Honeymoon*. © 1986 Orion Pictures Corporation.

The horror...the horror... Gilda Radner, Gene Wilder, and Dom DeLuise in
a publicity still for *Haunted Honeymoon*. © 1986 Orion Pictures Corporation.

Gene and Gilda at the 1986 U.S. Open in Flushing, New York, two months before Gilda was diagnosed with ovarian cancer. Photo by Barry Talesnick.

A dozen years after *Silver Streak,* Arthur Hiller again directed Gene Wilder in *See No Evil, Hear No Evil.* © 1989 Tri-Star Pictures, Inc.

Duffy Bergman (Gene Wilder) proposes to Meg Lloyd (Christine Lahti) in *Funny About Love.* © 1990 Paramount Pictures Corporation.

Gene Wilder attempts knocking some sense into Richard Pryor (apparently neither of them read the script) in *Another You.* © 1991 Tri-Star Pictures, Inc.

Father knows best. Hillary B. Smith and Gene Wilder (top, left to right); Ian Bottiglieri and Carl Michael Lindner (front, left to right) in a publicity shot for *Something Wilder.* © 1994 National Broadcasting Company, Inc.

Happiness at last. Gene and fourth wife Karen, of whom he says "I am desperately in love with." Photo by Chris Preovolos, *The Stamford Advocate*. © 2008 Southern Conn. Newspapers, Inc.

# 18

# Not Another Hit

After the success of *See No Evil, Hear No Evil,* Gene Wilder and Richard Pryor didn't waste much time before teaming up again. Their fourth film together was called *Another You.* Like *See No Evil, Hear No Evil,* it was released by Tri-Star Pictures. *Another You* went into production with Peter Bogdanovich directing, but the mistaken identity comedy was beset with problems early on and Bogdanovich soon left the film. He was replaced by a less experienced director named Maurice Phillips.

In the film, Gene plays George, a just released sanitarium patient who ex-con Eddie (Pryor), as part of his community service, must help readjust to society. But George is a compulsive liar who just cannot stop lying once he starts. When George is mistaken for a long-lost beer tycoon named Abe Fielding, Eddie convinces George to play along so he can take advantage of Fielding's money, his estate, and his beautiful wife (Mercedes Ruehl).

*Another You* opened on July 26, 1991 and, unlike the three previous Wilder-Pryor outings, was a box-office disaster. The film cost $17 million to make and grossed a meager $2.8 million. Tri-Star did not screen the film in advance for critics, which is always a sign that a studio has little faith in its product.

The critics were unanimous in their disdain for the film and almost all of them made mention of how physically weak Pryor looked on-screen. Stephen Holden of *The New York Times* called it "frantically incoherent" and "so choppily put together that it has no internal momentum." Terry Kelleher of *Newsday* wrote, "Casual observers of Peter Bogdanovich's career may think he hasn't caught a break in quite a while. The director has at least one thing to be grateful for, however: He was relieved of his duties on *Another You*." Kelleher also noted, "When he's not doing the liar number, Wilder goes into his usual 'love me, I'm having a panic attack' mode. The saddest thing about this desperate comedy is Pryor's minimal contribution. Given little to do but stand ready and slur an occasional vulgarism, the co-star seems to be having no more fun than the audience." "There isn't a single laugh in *Another You*," Gene Siskel said. "Both Richard Pryor and Gene Wilder, of course, have had to deal with well publicized health problems recently, and maybe this picture was therapeutic for them. But they got paid millions for their work and now we're being asked to pay it back. It's not fair. These guys are so much better than this miserable script."

Had Gene Wilder and Richard Pryor not done *Another You*, their collective work together would have made for a great track record. *Another You* was clearly not worthy of their talent and it baffled many as to what they could have possibly found redeeming in the screenplay by Ziggy Steinberg, whose name seems to muster more laughs than his script did.

If anything good came out of *Another You*, it was that its Hollywood premiere raised $100,000 for the Gilda Radner Ovarian Cancer Detection Center, which Gene established at Cedars-Sinai Medical Center in Los Angeles.

Though Wilder and Pryor did not socialize when they weren't working together, they seemed to see more of each other off the set while doing *See No Evil, Hear No Evil* and *Another You*. During both of these films, Pryor appeared less volatile and more subdued, perhaps because of his failing health. Although most everyone thought Pryor had kicked his longtime drug habit, he was still using, as well as drinking heavily, to dull both the physical and mental strain of his MS.

Gene was too polite to say that the real reason he could not connect with Pryor in real life was because Pryor was a hardcore drug addict who, while sometimes gentle and sweet, was more often paranoid and irrational. During publicity for *Another You*, Gene gave a tepid theory as to why they never became close friends offscreen: "If we would see each other and go to a movie, go to dinner — oh, we did once in a while — but I mean if we would do it regularly, then maybe an argument would start and maybe we'd start fighting like Abbott and Costello did."

"I'm not going to retire and shrivel up into a hole and not kiss anyone anymore."

— *Gene Wilder*

# 19

# In Love Again

Gilda loved Gene completely. Gene loved her, but not with the intensity and passion that Gilda had for him. Despite their outward persona of being the perfect Hollywood couple, it was a one-sided relationship. Gene was without question the great love of Gilda's life. She loved being Mrs. Gene Wilder, making sure to always sign her checks "Gilda Wilder," not "Gilda Radner." In fact, she rarely wanted to be apart from him.

Gene found Gilda extremely difficult to live with. Her neediness annoyed him and this often put a strain on the marriage. In addition, Gene had to put up with Gilda's bulimia, which got so bad that her teeth began to rot from throwing up so much. According to Gene, Gilda was also known to sometimes start the morning with a flask that contained vodka and Tab. "But it's quarter to eight in the morning," Gene would say. "It's just to calm my nerves a little bit," was Gilda's reply.

When Gene and Gilda met, they were both in rather precarious emotional states. She was in a marriage that wasn't working while he was still recovering from a breakup with a British drama student who was more than half his age. After they became a couple, Gilda told Gene that in the car ride into Manhattan from Connecticut on the first night of shooting *Hanky Panky*, she cried the entire way. When Gene asked her why, she admitted that she thought she would fall in love with him and they would eventually get married.

Gene and Gilda were two very different people. Gilda lived to perform. She constantly wanted to be in the public spotlight. Gene has always been very private and was never a big part of the Hollywood scene. Gilda used to try persuading Gene to let reporters come to their home to profile them for magazines, but Gene made it clear that was not his thing. Some of Gilda's friends felt that Gene stifled Gilda's career by making her become a homebody, but Gilda strived to make Gene happy, so she put aside her desire for the limelight by trying to lead the same quiet life Gene did.

When Connie Chung interviewed Gene in 1990, he said his time with Gilda was "the best years of my life." With Gilda dead only a year, Gene knew it would be damaging to his reputation and the myth of them as an ideal couple to say anything less. It would be fifteen years before he would admit in his memoir that although he and Gilda did have their share of good times, their marriage was far from the best years of his life.

One can only speculate what might have happened had Gilda not gotten sick, but it is unlikely that Gene would have been able to continue tolerating her neuroses. Once she was diagnosed with cancer, he felt he had to stay in the marriage, largely out of guilt for walking out on Jo and Katie twelve years earlier.

In the months following Gilda's death, Gene's relationship with Karen Webb developed into much more than friendship. "I didn't even see them becoming good friends," said Arthur Hiller. "I don't even remember her on the set more than twice…Did I feel a romance or something beginning? I didn't. I'm not saying it wasn't occurring, I'm just saying I sure didn't see [anything]."

A week before shooting wrapped on *See No Evil, Hear No Evil*, Karen invited Gene to her Manhattan apartment for dinner. Although Gene accepted her dinner offer, he initially had doubts since he was attracted to her and Gilda was still alive. Gene and Karen shared a brief kiss at the end of the evening, but it wasn't until several months after Gilda's death that they resumed contact after Karen enlisted Gene's aid on a public service video about the hard of hearing.

They met at Gene's favorite Italian restaurant in Manhattan. Karen brought a tape recorder and during their meal tried to show Gene some common problems people who are hard of hearing regularly encounter. Shortly afterwards, they had a second meeting at the same restaurant. The next time, Gene told Karen not to bring the recorder. Gene considers this their first real date. "Pretty soon those feelings started to become feelings of love on both sides," he said. "It was like spring, seeing the buds after a winter."

Gene was evasive on the subject of marrying again when the question was raised by interviewer Arthel Neville two months before he and Karen wed. He instead offered these profound words: "If someone dies that you're very close to, you can have two different reactions that I know of. One is, you go into a shell — well, you're going to go into a shell no matter what happens — but you stay in the shell and you become bitter about life and about people and about love and part of you dies. And other people — me — who've had love and someone dies and that person who died wants more than anything in the world for you to live and thinks that the greatest tragedy that can happen to any human being is [the loss of] their singularity, their uniqueness — the thing that makes Arthel Arthel and Gene Gene — the essence of it, though — not just the outer fringes, but the essence, whatever that is. If you're not being that and doing that every day of your life then you're missing out. And someone who's dying can tell you don't, please don't lose it. But most of us are walking around during the day and we're too busy with other things to realize that our lives are slipping away. Because when you're happy and when I'm happy is when we are most ourselves, when we can say, 'That's me. Yeah, that's me.' And when you feel yucky and crummy and shitty, you say, 'I didn't feel like I was myself, that wasn't me…' And Gilda's message was everyone should be who you really are as much of the day and night as you possibly can be. And in that sense, I'm full of life and love and ready for anything that could happen in my life. I'm not going to retire and shrivel up into a hole and not kiss anyone anymore."

On September 8, 1991 — ten days before what would have been Gene and Gilda's seventh wedding anniversary — Gene Wilder, 58, married Karen Webb (nee Boyer), 49, in the backyard of the

Connecticut home Gilda left Gene in her will. The couple honeymooned in England.

Karen was born on May 25, 1942 and is originally from the small, predominantly Mormon town of Arco, Idaho. She has one son, Kevin, from her previous marriage.

Gene discussed his decision to remarry with Joel Siegel, calling it "the most intuitive, natural — I don't know how to say — feeling of rightness that I've had in…maybe in all my life. I think if Gilda were to pick out anyone in the world that I know of, she would have picked out Karen for me as someone who would help me in my life now to live fully and happily."

When he was married to Gilda, if Gene wanted to go play tennis with some friends for a few hours, she would want to come along, otherwise she would want to know when he would be home — not uncommon behavior for a loving wife. The irony with his fourth marriage is that the constant companionship that he found so cloying with Gilda he embraces with Karen, who rarely ever leaves his side. She is very protective of Gene and accompanies him to every interview and talk show appearance, and actually sits at the table with him during book signings.

"She is the great love of my life," he said of Karen in the fall of 2000. "I only had Gilda for a short time. Being with Gilda was like being with a shooting star. I don't mean in terms of the shortness of her life — that, too — but just trying to hold on to her. Her spirit was always darting around. We were in love, but it was a different kind of love. It was a roller coaster and it was fun, but the marriage I have now is different. It's very peaceful, very passionate, very satisfying. It's difficult when two people are artists. It can work, but that's the exception to the rule because both people have this burning [desire] to have the spotlight on them, and it doesn't make for peaceful Sunday mornings," he said with a grin.

"I was very unhappy for a long while with Gilda," Gene admitted to interviewer Ernie Manouse, "and I'm happier now than I've ever been in my life…I didn't think I'd ever get married again. And I didn't believe in fate either. I always felt you make your own life and then call it fate. With Karen…" Gene began to tear up. "I do believe in fate."

"With all the great medical care I was receiving, and all the support from my family and friends, there was still something missing: *None of those people had cancer.*"

— *Gilda Radner*

# 20

# Welcome to the Club

In May 1991, Joanna Bull came to New York to meet with Gene Wilder, Joel Siegel, and Mandy Patinkin. They got together to begin the process of establishing Gilda's Club, a free-of-charge support community for people with cancer and their friends and family modeled after The Wellness Community. A four-story brownstone on West Houston Street that was formerly an 11,700 square foot furniture showroom is the home to Gilda's Club. Gilda's Club got off the ground with the help of many of Gilda's friends and colleagues, as well as many generous contributions from corporations and private citizens. Through special events, such as 5K walks and tennis tournaments, Gilda's Club raised money to renovate the actual edifice, as well as to fund the yearly operating costs. Additional support continues to come from a number of celebrities on Gilda's Club's honorary board, including Mel Brooks, Carol Burnett, Jane Curtin, Rick Moranis, Matilda Cuomo, and Joan Rivers. The clubhouse officially opened on June 13, 1995.

Joel Siegel served as president of Gilda's Club until his death in 2007, and like Gene, had his own personal reasons for helping found the club, having also lost a wife to cancer. "Medical science works on keeping you from dying," Siegel said. "That's what chemotherapy does, that's what intensive care does. Something like this keeps you living."

"We see Gilda's Club as being a part of total cancer treatment," said Joanna Bull. She also believes that cancer patients need to feel that they aren't totally helpless. The word "victim" is never used at Gilda's Club. "One of the first things that people feel when they're diagnosed with cancer is that their whole lives are completely out of control," Bull said. "Everything that will happen at Gilda's Club will be designed to bring back that sense of control."

In addition to the services it offers in New York City, Gilda's Club quickly initiated a training program for counselors and has since branched out throughout North America and Europe, not unlike what the Ronald McDonald Houses have done. Currently there are Gilda's Clubs in Florida, Detroit, Chicago, Ohio, Nashville, New Jersey, Wisconsin, Texas, Montreal, Toronto, and London, to name a few.

From the secret garden on the roof to "Noogieland," a playroom where children and teenagers can spend time with or without their parents, Gilda's Club, like its West Coast inspiration, offers cancer patients a place they can go to and know they're not alone. "We're calling it Gilda's Club because I think that's what Gilda would have wanted it to be called," Gene said. "Not something that scares you away. Something happy, some place where you could look forward to going."

It would be pessimistic to the point of futility to speculate that Gene founded Gilda's Club out of guilt for not loving Gilda the same way that she loved him. He witnessed firsthand how The Wellness Community lifted Gilda's spirits when she was at her lowest point. He knew Gilda would have wanted him to do this, saying, "I don't think she'd say, 'Thank you, darling.' I think she'd say, 'It's about time.'" Karen supported Gene in his efforts with Gilda's Club and also pitched in to help, never having any qualms about living in the shadow of a famous deceased wife. Whatever Gene's motives were — and having spent the first two years after Gilda's death promoting ovarian cancer detection, there is no reason to believe those motives were not genuine — the end result is that thanks to him, Gilda's Club provides comfort to untold numbers of cancer patients and their families all over the world when there seems little hope at all.

In 2002 Gene was honored for his work with Gilda's Club at the Cosmetic Executive Women's Beauty Awards. Rosie O'Donnell emceed the event at the Waldorf-Astoria Hotel in New York City and presented Gene with the first ever Roche Beauty of Giving Award, sponsored by the Roche pharmaceutical company. While accepting the award, Gene urged everyone in the audience to read O'Donnell's book *Find Me,* in which she talks about her mother's death from breast cancer. After reading it, Gene said, "I felt as if I had a little sister."

In recent years Gene Wilder and Joanna Bull have taken less active roles in Gilda's Club. While they both remain on the board of directors, Bull is no longer the club's executive director and Gene no longer serves as vice president. For Gene, it simply seemed like time to move on. "I was getting to be known as Mr. Cancer,'" Gene said. "I thought, 'Get back to your life and start working again.'"

"I've contemplated doing a television series for at least eighteen seconds."

— *Gene Wilder*

# 21

# Not Ready for Prime Time

The failure of *Another You* made Gene Wilder realize that formulas don't always work. While two years earlier moviegoers rushed to *See No Evil, Hear No Evil*, the fourth Wilder-Pryor pairing didn't even make enough money at the box office to break the top ten for that weekend. In an interesting side note, Mel Brooks' film *Life Stinks*, which opened the same day, also failed to make the top ten. So it seemed that Gene Wilder and Mel Brooks, two stars whose names usually meant big box office in the 1970s, now couldn't draw the crowds in.

Brooks would direct two more films before abandoning movies for the Broadway stage, while Gene decided to give the small screen a shot. He had once said, when talking about comedians such as Sid Caesar whose career fizzled too soon, "The thought of having my work cut short by the fickleness of public taste, or because of some frailty in my own creativity — now that terrifies me." So, after two box-office bombs in a row, Gene Wilder agreed to star in a pilot for NBC called *Eligible Dentist*.

Though this was Gene's first foray into TV sitcoms, he had done television before. In the 1960s, he did a commercial for Gillette razors, voiceovers for two animated Alka-Seltzer commercials, and the voiceover for a live-action V8 juice commercial. In addition to the work he did on such '60s programs as NBC's *The DuPont Show of the Week* and CBS's *The Defenders*, he also appeared in a 1972 comedy special on NBC called *The Trouble With People*, which co-starred George C. Scott, Renee Taylor, Alan Arkin, and Valerie Harper in five sketches written by Neil Simon. In 1972 he played Lord Ravensbane in a public television production of Percy MacKaye's play *The Scarecrow*. The witchcraft drama, which won an Emmy Award for art direction, co-starred Elisha Cook, Norman Lloyd, Blythe Danner, and Nina Foch. In 1973 he played opposite Marlo Thomas in an ABC special entitled *Acts of Love — And Other Comedies*, written by Joseph Bologna and Renee Taylor and directed by Charles Grodin. Gene also appeared on Anne Bancroft's 1974 ABC variety special *Annie and the Hoods* along with Mel Brooks, Carl Reiner, Jack Benny, Alan Alda, Tony Curtis, and Robert Merrill. From 1972-1977, Gene was the voice of the animated superhero Letterman on the PBS children's show *The Electric Company*, and in 1980 he appeared on five episodes of another educational PBS show, *3-2-1 Contact*, in which, among other things, he illustrated communication by talking to a dog. Other guest spots he has done include *Baryshnikov in Hollywood*, a 1982 variety special, and *A Party for Richard Pryor*, a televised 1991 tribute.

*Eligible Dentist* was yet another in a long series of shows showcasing sixtyish film stars who hadn't had theatrical hits in a while, such as Faye Dunaway and Dudley Moore, both of whom starred in short-lived situation comedies around this time.

The premise of *Eligible Dentist* was simple enough: a recently widowed tooth doc deals with an array of office loonies while trying his hand at dating in the '90s. The impressive cast included two of Gene's former leading ladies, Jill Clayburgh and Carol Kane, as well as Mary Gross and Wallace Shawn. With all of these names, one would think this show would have a pretty good chance for success, but reactions to test viewings were so negative that NBC never even aired the pilot episode.

But Gene Wilder's television career did not end with *Eligible Dentist*. Instead, NBC gave him another series, and this time they aired it. Originally called *Young at Heart*, the show's mundane title was changed to the snappier *Something Wilder*. The show was

created by Lee Kalcheim, who wrote for *All in the Family*, and
Barnet Kellman, who was one of the producers and directors of
*Murphy Brown*. *Something Wilder* was a family series in the truest
sense, a good-natured comedy about a husband and wife and their
two cute kids. Like most actors who have their names in the show
title, Gene and his character shared the same first name. He was
Gene Bergman, a nice guy with a much younger wife named Annie
(Hillary B. Smith of daytime's *One Life to Live*) and a set of preco-
cious twin boys named Sam and Gabe (Ian Bottiglieri and Carl
Michael Lindner), who bear a remarkable resemblance to their on-
screen father. They've just moved from the hustle-bustle of New
York to tranquil and suburban Stockbridge, Massachusetts where
Gene and his friend Jack (Gregory Itzin) run an advertising agency
out of a barn behind Gene's country home.

"The series is a chance for me to do the kind of comedy I can't
do in the movies," Gene said. "I think it's a compliment if someone
calls my comedy 'old-fashioned.' I love physical comedy the best,
but it has to have a reason behind it. I prize a cheap physical gag."

The show ran into problems early on when Jennifer Grey, who
was originally cast as Annie, was replaced after several episodes
when producers realized she looked just too young to play Gene's
wife.

The debut episode of *Something Wilder* dealt with Gene and
Annie's angst over Sam and Gabe starting preschool. Subsequent
episodes tended to deal with the same theme of Gene trying to be
as active and youthful a father as possible, despite his age, such as in
the second episode in which Gene agrees to coach Sam and Gabe's
soccer team, only to realize he's not as physically fit as he thought.
So he goes shopping for a NordicTrack and throws his back out
while testing it, something he tries hiding from Annie.

More memorable episodes had Gene trying to cover up getting
chocolate all over Jack's new white sofa, a gag stolen straight out
of one of Gene's movies, *The Adventure of Sherlock Holmes' Smarter
Brother*, but funny nonetheless. Mistaken identity was played to
the hilt in the episode entitled "Dr. Roof," where Wallace Shawn
guest starred as a roofing contractor Gene and Annie think is
a child psychologist. And Gene had a classic moment when he

tried getting a tired actor in a dog suit to perform at Sam and Gabe's birthday party. The actor locks himself in a men's room stall and refuses to go to the twins' party. As Gene begs him "to come out of there and perform the act you promised," someone walks into the restroom and thinks Gene has just paid the guy in the stall for sex.

The first episode of *Something Wilder* aired on Saturday, October 1, 1994 at 8:00 p.m. The show had a delightful opening credits sequence in which Gene and his family paint over the screen as Gene sings "You Brought a New Kind of Love to Me," a charming 1930 pop song written by Sammy Fain, Irving Kahal, and Pierre Norman Connor. Unfortunately, the entire opening sequence was scrapped after a few episodes. The show finished in 88th place with a dismal 5.7 rating/11 share during its first two weeks on the air. NBC soon moved the show from 8:00 to 8:30. It followed the long-running *Empty Nest*, which itself was not performing like it once did, and did little to help *Something Wilder's* ratings. After a six-week hiatus, NBC gave *Something Wilder* a second chance by moving it to Tuesdays at 8:30, sandwiching it between the hit shows *Wings* and *Frasier*. The ratings improved, but not enough. On its best week, the show finished in 30th place.

While it failed to draw big ratings, *Something Wilder* did muster some critical praise. *TV Guide's* Jeff Jarvis wrote, "Gene Wilder must have been an awfully cute kid, for he certainly turned into a cute grown-up. He looks like a male, middle-aged Shirley Temple with his curly locks and impishly innocent, kewpie-doll grin. He's impossible not to like." Jarvis called the show "a charming throwback to the early days of the sitcom. And on television, that's not easy to be: a throwback *and* charming...I'm not surprised that all these TV institutions — the happy family, the crazy neighbor lady — are coming back. I'm just a little surprised that it's Gene Wilder who's bringing them. In the movies...he was a crazed comic genius as tightly wound as his hair. But on television, he has managed to break his self-imposed typecasting and turn normal. He is just what TV needed: a funnyman, a nice guy, a good father."

*The Washington Post's* Tom Shales wrote in his review that the show "is no laugh riot, but it's sweet-natured, easy to take and easy to like…The frizzle-haired, frazzle-faced Wilder, whose movie career has apparently bottomed out, looks more than ever like a latter-day Harpo Marx. Very latter. Wilder isn't that late in life himself, but he looks it…It's gratifying to see an older actor admitting he's older, even if no specific age is mentioned…*Something Wilder* won't make anybody's list of most unforgettable TV series, unless Wilder himself has such a list. But its banality is comforting rather than irritating, and it's unlikely to send anybody running from the room screaming."

While *Something Wilder* — which on any given week featured such guest stars as Joey Lawrence, Michele Lee, Marla Maples Trump, and even rocker Alice Cooper — may not have reached great comic heights every episode, it did have a charm and gentle humor that many shows lack today. Had it been given the chance to continue, *Something Wilder* may have found its niche, but after fifteen episodes, the show was canceled, finishing in 66th place for the season.

Gene continued to stay away from feature films following the cancellation of *Something Wilder*, but he did return to the stage. It had been almost thirty years since he appeared in a play, but in the fall of 1996 he performed in a four-month run of Neil Simon's *Laughter on the 23rd Floor* at the Queen's Theatre in London's West End. In a role originated on Broadway by Nathan Lane, Gene played Max Prince, a Sid Caesar-like comedian who is the star of a 1950s TV program not unlike *Your Show of Shows*.

Gene has turned down offers to appear on Broadway due to what he feels is the current need for every new show to be an instant runaway hit. "I'm asked to do theatre in New York all the time," he said. "I haven't wanted to. I've wanted to do a play in London since 1975; that was conscious…In New York, it's hit or miss, and I thought, after all this time, I don't want a million-megaton hit or a disaster. In England, people go to the theatre. Maybe it will be a big hit, or a little hit. But the play's the thing, and I love the play, and I feel the people here will want to see me and want to see the play, as opposed to thinking, 'I hear that play's hard to get into; let's go to that.'"

*Laughter on the 23rd Floor* was a hit in London and received an Olivier Award nomination for Best New Comedy. The *News of the World* proclaimed it "the funniest night out in London," while *The Daily Telegraph* found it "both funny and genuinely touching." The *Daily Express* wrote, "Wilder is brilliant," and the *Daily Mail* called him "a 24-carat gold star."

Gene's next stage appearance after his stint in London was a one-night-only benefit performance of A.R. Gurney's two-character play *Love Letters* with Mary Tyler Moore on April 23, 1999 at the C.W. Post Campus of Long Island University in Brookville, New York. Despite ticket prices that ranged from $200 per person (which included entry into a pre-show cocktail hour) to $500 per person (which included the gala dinner after the show), the performance was a sellout. It raised money for the North Shore Child & Family Guidance Center, an agency based in Roslyn Heights, Long Island. Gene was asked to do the play by a friend who is one of the agency's board members.

"You can't be a television actor and a movie actor at the same time…except if you're Columbo. If you're born Columbo, you've got a small chance."

— *Gene Wilder*

# 22

# Such a
# Nice Jewish Detective

With the 1990s drawing to a close, Gene Wilder had only appeared in two feature films the whole decade, *Funny About Love* and *Another You*. But in 1999, after a long period of not doing any film work, Gene occupied himself with several projects, most notably *Murder in a Small Town*, a murder mystery he and his brother-in-law Gilbert Pearlman wrote for the A&E cable network (though this was the first time Gene and Gil collaborated on a film, Gil had written the novelizations of both *Young Frankenstein* and *The Adventure of Sherlock Holmes' Smarter Brother*).

The project evolved when, according to Gene, "Someone at A&E came to me and said, 'You think up a character — any character you like in a murder mystery...' I talked to my partner in this, Gilbert Pearlman, and we started thinking about what profession I might have and what the story would be about. I'm very good with writing dialogue and characters, and Gilbert is very good with creating the structure of a story, which is the hardest part for me."

An avid mystery fan, Gene welcomed the challenge of both writing one and taking on a role that wasn't necessarily comedic. "My wife, Karen and I, when we go to sleep at night, almost always tune in to see if there's a murder mystery on the air," Gene said. "It just takes you out of the world you've been in for the last fourteen, fifteen, sixteen hours. You can let your mind go and involve yourself in this murder that took place and try and figure out who did it. And it's refreshing afterwards, if it's a good one."

*Murder in a Small Town* is set in 1938 and stars Gene as Larry "Cash" Carter, a theater director who was nicknamed Cash by *Variety* after directing five runaway hits in a row on Broadway. After his wife is brutally murdered in front of him during a robbery, Cash retreats to the peace and quiet of Stamford, Connecticut to raise his daughter and run his own community theater. After a much hated local businessman named Sidney Lassiter (Terry O'Quinn) is murdered, Cash's good friend, Detective Tony Rossini (Mike Starr), asks him to assist in cracking the case, since Cash's insights into character development and the motivation of the criminal mind have proven invaluable to Tony in the past. The list of suspects is long. Was it Lassiter's ignored wife (Frances Conroy), who had to deal with the knowledge that her husband preferred prostitutes to her? Was it Lassiter's son (Matthew Edison), who puts on the facade of a swinging ladies' man to hide his true identity from his father? Was it Lassiter's longtime secretary (Deirdre O'Connell), whose relationship with Lassiter was at one point more than just business? Or did the butler do it?

While there are moments of humor in *Murder in a Small Town*, the film truly was a departure for Gene. This is a genuine murder mystery, not a comedy. Still, Cash is in many ways very much a Gene Wilder kind of character. Though not as manic or neurotic as most of the parts Gene has played, Cash, like Gene himself, is soft-spoken, funny, likable, and a romantic at heart. The latter is most evident in the scene where Cash serenades his girlfriend Mimi (Cherry Jones) with a concertina to the Rodgers and Hart tune "Mimi." He's also Jewish (the family name was changed to Carter from Kartofsky, he explains).

Joyce Chopra, whose previous films included *Smooth Talk* (1986) and *The Lemon Sisters* (1990), was chosen to direct, marking the first time Gene had been directed on-screen by a woman. According to producer Fred Berner, "There had always been sort of an underlying sensibility that it might be nice to have a woman director for this piece. I think we all felt it would add a nice touch of elegance and sensibility to it...She's got a tremendous understanding of the medium. She's able to do a movie in a short television schedule, but by the same token, what she brings to it is that same shared appreciation for elegance."

Though set in Gene's hometown of Stamford, *Murder in a Small Town* was actually filmed in Toronto, Canada. "There are more authentic streets, shops and movie theaters in Toronto," Gene told *TV Guide*. "And secondly, I went to the desk of the hotel and gave them $200 American. They gave me back $298 Canadian. If you switch the figure to $3 million, you get back an awful lot."

Gene's co-stars had nothing but praise for him. "I don't want to make any of the clichés of saying, 'Oh, it's just great. It's a dream come true.' 'Cause it's all of that, you know," said Mike Starr. "He's one of a kind, in his work and just as a guy. I can probably quote every line in *The Producers*, just to name one. Gene Wilder's multi-faceted and extremely helpful. He's a very hard-working man, and we also have a lot of laughs. I play the fan sometimes, you know. You don't want to be constantly bothering someone, so we work and have a good time and go out to dinner, but I just can't resist a few times quoting lines from various films. It's like, wow, sometimes I look and say, 'Hey, I'm with this guy.' I've been lucky to be with a lot of interesting people and he's right up there."

"I was surprised in rehearsing with Gene how funny I found him," said Terry O'Quinn. "I wasn't prepared for how ingenious Gene is. I think you can watch him [perform] and you can't help but smile. That's only happened to me once before, actually, and I thought about this when Gene was making me do it. I was on the stage once with Jessica Tandy and I wasn't prepared for how good she was. I started watching [her] and then I realized I was falling behind. Gene's kind of that way, you start watching him and you can't help but think that's pretty cool."

*Murder in a Small Town* premiered on A&E as the cable network's first original movie on January 10, 1999. The TV critics welcomed Gene's departure from his usual blend of screwball comedy and pondered the possibility of Gene using *Murder in a Small Town* as a springboard to becoming TV's next Columbo. "Gene Wilder might seem like an unlikely choice to play a quick-witted sleuth," wrote

*The New York Times'* Ron Wertheimer. "But that's just the point. Playing winningly against type, he makes a charming and surprisingly low-key amateur detective...Mr. Wilder, who has sanded the edges off his usual lunatic persona, has created an endearing hero: a little smart, a little nutsy, a little too good to be true. And just winning enough to be invited back." *People* magazine's Terry Kelleher wrote, "A good murder mystery should have surprises, and this TV movie offers a nice one: Gene Wilder's restrained performance... The script, co-written by Wilder, combines a competently plotted whodunit with almost too much information on the protagonist's personal life. It doesn't take a detective to guess that Wilder would like Cash to come back for another case or two. And there'd be no objection from this corner." *Newsday's* Steve Parks gave the film a mixed review. "Director Joyce Chopra handsomely renders the melange of late '30s show-biz and gumshoe atmospherics that Wilder's script, co-written with Gilbert Pearlman, evokes," wrote Parks. "But the screenplay, along with the film, loses its way in the buildup toward an unsupported surprise ending."

*Murder in a Small Town* was a ratings winner, so much so that after it aired, *Daily Variety's* John Dempsey reported that the "high ratings for *Murder in a Small Town* guarantee that A&E will do more movies starring Wilder as Cash Carter."

Six weeks after *Murder in a Small Town* premiered, Gene appeared in another TV movie, NBC's $21 million adaptation of Lewis Carroll's classic *Alice in Wonderland*. The all-star cast included Martin Short at the Mad Hatter, Whoopi Goldberg as the Cheshire Cat, and Ben Kingsley as Major Caterpillar. Gene played Mock Turtle, one of the many eccentric characters young Alice (Tina Majorino) encounters on her strange journey. As the aging half-man, half-turtle, Gene cracks corny jokes and sings and dances, bringing to mind his role as the Fox in *The Little Prince* twenty-five years earlier.

Gene felt this was a perfect role for him. "Everything I do, in the last, I don't know how many years," he said, "I've done because a bell goes off. When the bell goes off, I say, 'That's for me.' When I'm doing what I really know I should be doing with my life and my work, it's a feeling of satisfaction...He sings and dances, it's

SUCH A NICE JEWISH DETECTIVE     185

made for me. It didn't matter how big or small. I said, 'That's my part. It's my kind of stuff.'"

There had been many other screen versions of *Alice*, including a British one-reeler made in 1903, shortly after the advent of moving pictures; a 1933 production with W.C. Fields, Gary Cooper, and Cary Grant as Mock Turtle; Disney's 1951 animated version; and a 1985 telefilm produced by disaster movie king Irwin Allen. This *Alice*, which was filmed in London over a period of three months, took advantage of the strides computer generated special effects have made in recent years and contains some elaborate visuals, including several creations by Jim Henson's Creature Shop. For his ten-minute scene, Gene had to act in front of a blue screen. Alice and the character of Mock Turtle's friend the Gryphon were added later. "I've never done anything quite like it," Gene said. "Everything I did was not only against a blue screen, but also standing on a blue disc 10 feet wide...My acting teacher used to say acting was reacting to an imaginary stimulus."

*Alice in Wonderland* aired on February 28, 1999 and was the highest rated TV movie of the season, finishing as the fourth most watched program of that week and averaging a 14.8 rating (percentage of the nation's 99.4 million TV homes) and a 22 share (percentage of the sets in use), with an average 25,340,000 viewers. *Alice* won four Emmy Awards (for music, costume design, visual effects, and make-up) and also did well with the critics. The *New York Post* and New York *Daily News* both gave it four stars, while *Newsday*'s Steve Parks called it "the finest film treatment ever of this wondrous tale exploring the frighteningly intuitive, upside-down wisdom of innocence." Although Caryn James of *The New York Times* found *Alice* "flat," she did note it was "a triumph of design and smooth computer effects" and found Gene's performance "touching and funny."

The last time Gene Wilder appeared on-screen with Nazis, it was strictly for laughs. But in his second Cash Carter film for A&E, Gene found himself involved with Nazis who didn't raise pigeons or write Broadway musicals. The film was *The Lady in Question*, and once again Joyce Chopra directed from a script by Gene and Gil, whose original title was *Why Kill the Old Lady?*

The time is still 1938 and the place is still Stamford, Connecticut. Cash is in the midst of not only directing but also starring in a production of *Dinner at Eight* after his lead actor falls ill at the last minute. Cash's fiancée Mimi (Cherry Jones), a stewardess, is on her way back to Stamford from Germany. Onboard the plane, she meets Emma Sachs (Claire Bloom), a wealthy philanthropist whose work to help Jews escape the Holocaust has made her the most hated woman in Nazi Germany.

When the plane lands, Emma slips Mimi a note that simply reads "I'm going to be murdered." Once reunited with Cash, Mimi tells him of this odd gesture. Cash was an old acquaintance of Emma's, and her niece happens to be in Cash's current production, so he decides to look into the situation. When he shows up at Emma's house, her family informs him that Emma has just suffered a stroke and is barely clinging to life. Cash suspects foul play, however, and enlists his pal, Detective Tony Rossini (Mike Starr), to investigate. It turns out Emma was poisoned and thus begins the search for the killer from a group of suspects that includes several family members, Emma's traveling companion, and Emma's longtime maid.

*The Lady in Question* aired on A&E on December 12, 1999 and, like *Murder in a Small Town*, received positive notices from the critics, though they seemed to find the characters and performances more worthwhile than the actual plot. "Whodunit…is not as interesting as who solves it," wrote Robert Bianco in *USA Today*. "Wilder's Carter is an enjoyably intuitive sleuth, and his assistants are even more entertaining…As a writer, Wilder hasn't come up with a complicated enough mystery to solve. But as a performer, and with an able assist from Jones and Starr, he makes up for the story's flaws." *Daily Variety's* Ray Richmond gave *The Lady in Question* a rave. "Comedy icon Gene Wilder has turned gumshoe," Richmond wrote, "and he suddenly has a film franchise to call his own. The rejuvenated and enormously talented Wilder takes a second turn as Broadway-director-turned-amateur sleuth Larry 'Cash' Carter in *The Lady in Question*, with the resulting mystery even better than January's *Murder in a Small Town*…Carter is something of a cultured Lt. Columbo — eccentric, relentless, complex, explosive and wily — a character deserving of Wilder's efforts…Wilder's best moments come when he's allowed to rant and rave with obnoxious abandon. No one has the gift to work himself into an embarrassing, mouth-frothing frenzy quite like he can...It doesn't really matter that *Lady* is somewhat simple to unravel, playing less like a true whodunit and more like a 'how-to-catch-'em' (indeed, like *Columbo* before it)...While Wilder got only one shot playing a Broadway producer, it looks like he'll be back in the spotlight for a good long while playing a director."

Though A&E had originally intended to produce more Cash Carter films, new owners of the cable network shelved the idea. "I guess [the new owners] don't like murder mysteries," Gene said. "I think they need to have their heads examined."

JAMES LIPTON: What is your least favorite word?
GENE WILDER: Cancer.

— Inside the Actors Studio *(1996)*

# 23

# A Private Battle

With three successful TV movies in a row, 1999 was a productive year for Gene Wilder, but his professional achievements were overshadowed by the death of Madeline Kahn on December 3, 1999. Kahn publicly acknowledged her yearlong fight against ovarian cancer shortly before succumbing to the disease at age fifty-seven. Some of Gene's funniest moments on film were with Kahn, and with her, Dom DeLuise, Marty Feldman, and Harvey Korman gone, gone too is the hope that many Mel Brooks fans had that Brooks might make one more movie with his '70s regulars.

If it seemed a sad irony that the two women Gene Wilder is most associated having starred with on-screen both died of the same horrible disease, there was an even sadder irony, one Gene managed to keep secret for six months: he himself was fighting cancer. In August 1999, Gene was diagnosed with non-Hodgkin's lymphoma, the same lymph-system cancer that Jacqueline Kennedy Onassis died of. Lymphoma comes in two basic forms: Hodgkin's disease and non-Hodgkin's lymphoma, the latter being more common with an estimated 64,000 new cases diagnosed in 1999.

"There's an enormous selection of different lymphomas, literally dozens," said Dr. Mark Pasmantier of New York Presbyterian

Hospital. "And there are multiple kinds of treatments. The state, and what's called the histology, determines the treatment."

Gene's course of treatment was conventional chemotherapy. Considering all the different types of cancer that exist, Dr. Pasmantier said "lymphoma is one of the best to have because people live the longest. There are people who live years and years."

Though Gene maintains an active, healthy lifestyle (one friend proclaimed him "a real health nut"), he does have a family history of cancer. His father died of the disease and both his mother and sister had breast cancer, the latter having successfully fought it. As he had done for Gilda, Karen served as Gene's source of support and comfort during this difficult time. "You want her in your lifeboat," said one close friend of the couple.

Gene's chemotherapy treatment proved effective and after just five sessions he was in remission. On Sunday, January 30, 2000, Gene checked into Memorial Sloan-Kettering Cancer Center in New York for stem-cell replacement, a grueling procedure not unlike a bone marrow transplant, though obtaining stem cells does not involve actual surgery or general anesthesia. Stem cells are cells capable of regenerating normal bone marrow function. These cells were previously only obtainable from the patient's bone marrow, but stem-cell transplantation, a relatively new procedure in 2000, uses stem cells that are removed from the patient's blood, then frozen until the patient is ready for their reinfusion to replace cells destroyed by chemotherapy and restore the blood and immune systems.

Though he was in remission, non-Hodgkin's lymphoma has a high rate of recurrence, so, at the urging of a doctor in California who had treated Gilda, Gene opted to have the procedure as preventive treatment. Joanna Bull called Gene's decision to undergo stem-cell replacement "very positive and smart. It has an excellent track record."

A drug called G-CSF, which was discovered at Sloan-Kettering in the 1980s, reduces the risk of infection and, according to Dr. Stephen Nimer, director of the Division of Hematologic Oncology at Sloan-Kettering, "This drug makes collecting stem cells easier and greatly enhances the number of stem cells collected."

News of Gene Wilder having cancer was reported in the print and television media on February 4, 2000, following word that the supermarket tabloid the *Star* was going to run a story about Gene having the disease. The *Star* made no mention of what kind of cancer Gene had, nor did it mention that he was in remission. And, not surprisingly, they chose to put a rather unflattering picture of Gene, looking dazed and tired, on the cover, proclaiming "Gene Wilder battling cancer — disease killed wife Gilda."

The weekend before he checked into Sloan-Kettering for the stem-cell transplant, Gene was in Scottsdale, Arizona for a little vacation. He was enjoying a couple of beers in the bar of the Hyatt Regency Hotel with some friends during a karaoke night. He was particularly taken with a young Texas woman named Bonnie Hunter, who was in town celebrating her birthday with her father. After she sang a couple of numbers, Gene approached her.

"He said he really liked my voice and that he thought it refreshing that I sounded more country than anything else," said Hunter. "He looked very familiar to me…both his smile and his voice but I couldn't place him. He asked my name. I told him that my name was Bonnie, and he said, 'It's a pleasure to meet you, Bonnie, I am Gene Wilder.' I about died right there. *Of course it was him!* He was really the nicest man, and as I was leaving I spoke to him for another few minutes. He hugged me and wished me a happy birthday and then we parted."

According to the *Star*, an "eyewitness" said Gene looked "really bad" when he checked into Sloan-Kettering. "His face was puffy and swollen and he had a stocking cap pulled so far down over his head, it was practically covering his eyebrows," claimed the source. "Gene Wilder is known for his bushy hair, but it looked like he didn't have any hair at all under that hat."

Bonnie Hunter dispelled the *Star*'s "eyewitness report." "I wouldn't say he looked really bad," said Hunter. "He was smiling and happy and enjoying the music and having a beer…[My dad] said that Gene looked like he had gained quite a bit of weight…" Though Gene did initially lose his hair as a result of chemotherapy, Bonnie Hunter noted that, "His hair was quite longer too."

Having been through the ordeal of losing Gilda to cancer and then devoting himself to getting the word out about early cancer detection, news that Gene Wilder now had the disease caused great concern among his fans. "He's out of the hospital, he's still in remission, and he's doing very well," said close friend Susan Ruskin on March 8, 2000. "The newspapers really blew it out of proportion."

Perhaps no newspaper blew it out of proportion quite the way the *New York Post* did. On September 15, 2000, in an article about the Broadway version of *The Producers*, Page Six editor Richard Johnson wrote, "Nathan Lane's co-star in *Springtime for Hitler* will be Matthew Broderick, in the role made famous by the late Gene Wilder." The following day, the *Post* printed a correction, but rival gossip columnist Mitchell Fink of the *Daily News* couldn't resist chiming in, calling the error "completely foolish." Two years later, the *Post* made the same error, again referring to Gene as "the late actor" in a January 2, 2003 article about Roger Bart taking over the Leo Bloom role in *The Producers*.

Having been cancer-free for over a decade, Gene acknowledges that he is one of the "lucky ones." He tries not to let trivial things — even false reports of his death — get to him. "Things can happen that would have been upsetting before, but now I say I have everything a man could want: love, health and enough money to live on so I can just work on what I feel passionately about," he said in the fall of 2000. "I have no complaints about anything."

"When I was a kid, I was quite inhibited in life, in real life," Gene said in 2001. "But not onstage. Now I'm not afraid of anything. Since having cancer, I'm not afraid of hardly anything."

"I'm quietly political. I don't like advertising. Giving money to someone or support, but not getting on a bandstand. I don't want to run for president in 2008. I will write another book instead."

— *Gene Wilder*

# 24

# God and Politics

Unlike many friends and colleagues like Warren Beatty, Jane Fonda, Charles Grodin, and Donald Sutherland, Gene Wilder has never been outspoken politically, though in the 1960s, along with Elaine May and Renee Taylor, he did campaign for such liberal Democrats as Eugene McCarthy, Allard Lowenstein, and Paul O'Dwyer. He and Karen are both registered to vote in Connecticut, but neither is affiliated with a political party. On most issues, though, Gene, like most of his colleagues, tends to lean left. He was a fierce opponent of the Vietnam War and still holds a great deal of contempt for President George W. Bush and his decision to invade Iraq.

When asked by Tom Gogola in an interview for *Fairfield County Weekly* in the fall of 2006 if he thought Bush was good at playing stupid, Gene answered, "I don't think he's playing at being stupid. I'm not commenting on whether or not he's a nice man, because I wouldn't have any idea — oh, dear, I don't want to turn into a political polemicist right now, but I carry a certain amount of anger in me for all the people, Iraqis and American soldiers who have died because he decided to go into Iraq and invade it on a false premise, and led us all to believe there were weapons of mass destruction. All those people are dead, and you can't bring them back..."

"How could you possibly live with yourself if you knew the truth? You have to believe your own lies; I don't know how you can life [sic] with yourself with 2,800 dead: You have to say it was the right thing to do. To have that on your conscience, that you killed so many people — that's what I can't forgive Bush for. He might be nice with his wife and his dog and his children; my opinion is based only on Iraq."

In 2007 Gene said he hoped the next president would be a Democrat. He donated $2,300 to Barack Obama's campaign, although he expressed doubt about whether America was ready for a black president. "I like Barack Obama," he said. "I think he has a chance. It'll be difficult. It would be a great move forward for the US. But he isn't being guarded for no reason."

Gene also supports the Democrats because of most pro-life Republicans' opposition to embryonic stem cell research. "I saw Christopher Reeve at the US Open tennis championships in 2004," he said. "I told him 'I had a stem-cell transplant.' He was going to have an embryonic one in two months time, in another country and he died six weeks later. It's insane. The lives that could be saved."

Gene is an atheist, although as an adolescent he had what he described as a compulsion to constantly pray. He even admitted that when he had auditioned for the Actors Studio, he went to St. Patrick's Cathedral in New York and prayed to get in. "Not being Catholic, it was a little strange for a Jewish boy to go into St. Pat's and pray to get into the Actors Studio," he said, "but I wanted to cover all the bases."

In interviews where he has been asked about his faith, Gene never directly declared being an atheist or agnostic, though that could certainly be implied from his answers. When Larry King asked him if he believed in a higher power, Gene said, "You asked Stephen Hawking this once and he said, 'If by God you mean the mathematical equation that accounts for the creation of the solar systems and the black hole, yes, I do believe.' I would give the same answer." When Gene appeared on Bravo's *Inside the Actor's Studio* in 1996, host James Lipton posed his customary last question to Gene: "Gene, if heaven exists, what would you like to hear God say when you arrive?" Gene prefaced his answer with, "Well, I think that heaven does exist. It exists here and now. I don't know about later." As for what he would like to hear God say to him, he said, "Hi, honey. Want a cup of tea?"

Although as an adult Gene has always been proud of his Jewish heritage, growing up he was often embarrassed by it. "For example, if some Jew was too loud when I was nine years old..." he said, "I might say, 'How can I get out of here...Or if my Grandmas [sic] would kiss me in a certain place and all the kids were watching."

Of Gene's four wives, only Gilda was Jewish. "I married a Catholic, then I married another Catholic, and then I married Gilda — she's as Jewish as they come," he told Abigail Pogrebin in 2005 when she interviewed him for her book *Stars of David: Prominent Jews Talk About Being Jewish*. "She was pretty young, but she talked like an old Jew. And her jokes and her kvetching — it would have been easier to take, but it was so *Jewish* when it came out. I used to say, 'Do I have to listen to you kvetch in Jewish?'"

Gene attended an Orthodox temple that his grandfather was president of and, as is the Jewish tradition, he was bar mitzvahed when he was thirteen. "When I was BarMitzvahed [sic] — here's a story — they forgot to turn the microphone on," he recalled, "and it was one of the most heart-breaking [sic] experiences of my life. I had a very nice soprano voice — it hadn't changed yet — and but you couldn't here [sic] me if I sang Soprano [sic], so I had to sing low and it destroyed all the music that I had been working all year on. And I said, 'Those Jews, I'll kill them!' And this was at my BarMitzvah [sic], yet."

In 2005 Gene finally publicly "came out" as an atheist. "I'm going to tell you what my religion is," he told Pogrebin. "Do unto others as you would have them do unto you. Period. Terminato. *Finito*...I have no other religion. I feel very Jewish and I feel very grateful to be Jewish. But I don't believe in God or anything to do with the Jewish religion."

"I don't like show business. I like show. But I don't like the business."

— *Gene Wilder*

# 25

# Connecticut:
# Peace and Tranquility

Though it's been about thirty years or so since Gene Wilder was at the very top of his game, he still has a very devoted following, especially among women. "It overwhelms me the number of letters I get on a romantic level," Gene once said. "Nearly all my fan mail comes from girls between the ages of fifteen and thirty. I don't mind when they ask for an autographed picture, but telling me about the loneliness in their lives is something else. I take that very seriously which is why I dare not respond to most of the letters I get. That kind of fantasizing where I am the answer to their romantic problems could get serious if I were to write them a letter. I made that mistake twice. It would be understandable to respond to a letter like that because I am affected by it, but I must not or the results might be disastrous."

Gene is the first to acknowledge that he's never looked like the typical Robert Redford type leading man, and has admitted that he secretly would have liked to have been Louis Jourdan. He credits Alan Arkin and Dustin Hoffman for paving the way for unconventional looking guys like himself being taken seriously as leading men. "Arkin and Hoffman proved to the 'money people' what the creative people *already* knew — that they didn't need big names or matinee idol types to make successful movies," Gene said.

Gene's looks have earned him varying remarks from critics and journalists. "His face looks like a coconut on which someone has drawn a pair of blue eyes and pasted a Harpo wig," wrote Vincent Canby in his review of *The World's Greatest Lover*. "He hasn't become handsome exactly, but he's certainly sexy," wrote Barbara Bauer in 1977. Patricia Nolan described him as "handsome...with sparkling, intense blue eyes," while Jacqui Nicholson called him "ugly-handsome" with a "nose that looks like uncooked pasta" and a face that "reminds audiences of the comic giants of the past like Buster Keaton and Harold Lloyd."

Gene's trademark frizzy blond hair has earned him such comments as "mop-haired," "a latter-day Harpo Marx," and "a male, middle-aged Shirley Temple." "When I was a little boy, I don't even remember having curly hair," he has said. "I had wavy hair and wore it with a part. I still switch around sometimes. Something happened since *Blazing Saddles*. In *Young Frankenstein*, I wore it very long and with a part. It seems to have gotten curlier and curlier. I don't know. I think I look a little funny when I try to cut it and part it." In recent years, Gene has developed a bald spot, and after losing his hair as a result of chemotherapy, his hair has since grown back noticeably thinner and straighter ("wispy" is the word Bruce Weber used in *The New York Times*).

In 1975 a Baltimore woman named Judy Nathanson started the Gene Wilder International Fan Club and put out a quarterly fan club journal called *Geneology* that featured rather elaborate drawings of Gene, as well as articles, letters, and contributions from fans, nearly all of whom were female and openly gushed about their idol. Before the club dissolved in 1981, Nathanson and Christine Gardener put out a 50-page book of poetry and drawings inspired by Gene's characters called *A Touch of Madness*, which was sold through the fan club for $3.00.

According to John A. Simone Jr., who used to operate a Gene Wilder tribute Web site, "I have found that Gene Wilder has a very loyal international cult following. But what struck me as remarkable is that his fans are of a very intelligent and generous nature."

Gene Wilder has been compared to Woody Allen and Danny Kaye, and has even been called "America's Peter Sellers," though

Pauline Kael observed he "seems an inspired original, as peculiarly, elusively demented in his own way as the greatest original of them all, Jonathan Winters. You can't tell what makes clowns like this funny...Like Winters, Wilder taps a private madness."

Those who only think of Gene Wilder for his on-screen craziness are often surprised to see how erudite and philosophical he is in interviews. He feels every decision a person makes, no matter how small, can very well change the course of their life. "I stepped out in front of the Plaza Hotel one day after Gilda died," he recalled. "I could have gone around [the fountain] to the left or to the right. I stood there for a while and I said, 'I know what that means.' If I go to the left, my life will be different — could be different — than if I go to the right; and if I go to the right, vice versa. One little ripple changes everything else."

For Gene, those ripples are encompassed in his belief that if he didn't make the simple choice to do *Hanky Panky* to work with Sidney Poitier, he wouldn't have met Gilda, and indeed if he chose not to do *See No Evil, Hear No Evil*, he wouldn't now be married to Karen.

Tennis is one of Gene's great loves in life, and over the years he has participated in numerous celebrity tennis tournaments for charity. Gene has been quite athletic his entire adulthood, managing to keep his 5'10" frame lean, something that may stem from being overweight as a young child. "I was not fat," Gene said, "but I was chubby. But when I was called fatso, it left a big scar. So I've always felt not fat, but chubby most of my life, but not neurotically so."

Gene appreciates fine food and is himself a good cook. "When he's at home he likes to cook chicken," according to Gene's longtime secretary Kate Kovacs. When Martha Stewart asked Gene who does most of the cooking at home, he told her, "We share. Karen and I share. If it's something really simple like a leg of lamb or a roast chicken or a steak or the one that she likes best that I do is Poulet au Vinaigre — vinegar chicken — but with balsamic vinegar. Otherwise, if it has to do with a recipe or anything complicated, she makes it." He avoids junk food, rarely eats between meals, and tends to eat light lunches — cottage cheese, some salad, maybe some tuna (he and Gilda had a shared passion for tuna fish, which Gilda ate for lunch every day). He also enjoys dining out. A favorite local spot is a Japanese restaurant in Stamford called Kotobuki, a very casual and unpretentious sushi joint that doesn't look like the kind of place where a movie star might hang out (in Gene's honor, the restaurant named a sushi roll after him, the Gene-san roll, consisting of tuna, asparagus, and mayonnaise).

Over the years Gene has been involved with a number of projects that never got off the ground. After *Young Frankenstein*, Gene and Mel Brooks talked about doing another horror spoof, this time of *Dr. Jekyll & Mr. Hyde*, but the film never got beyond the development stage. Also, with Gene now directing, Brooks was casting himself as the lead in his own films. According to Gene, Brooks liked being a movie star, so, while their friendship never faltered, their creative partnership ended with *Young Frankenstein*.

In the late '70s, Gene set up his own production company and, in gratitude to the man who gave him his big break, called it Pal-Mel Productions. He intended to make Pal-Mel's first film *The Naked Lady*, a screenplay he wrote and planned on directing and starring in along with French actor Pierre Richard, but he abandoned that project (Gene officially dissolved Pal-Mel in the early '90s.) *Alone With My Girl*, a comedy he was writing with Ronny Graham, also never made it to the screen. Other screenplay ideas Gene had that never got made are *Double Whoopee* (original title *All Day Suckers*), *Dying for a Laugh* (original title *A Barrel of Money*), *Henry Orlow*, *Hold the Baby*, and *Tough Guy*.

After *The Frisco Kid*, producer Mace Neufeld had Gene in mind to star in a remake of the 1944 Dick Powell-Linda Darnell film *It Happened Tomorrow*, but the film never got made. Gene was in negotiations with Miramax Films to play Freddie Prinze Jr.'s father in *Down to You* (2000), but that deal fell through and the role went to Henry Winkler. Gene was set to lend his voice to Snowbell, the family cat, in *Stuart Little* (1999), but, despite actually doing the voiceover work, was replaced at the last minute by Nathan Lane. Columbia Pictures refused to comment on why Gene was replaced, but according to gossip columnist Ted Casablanca, "he was replaced by Lane when his work wasn't bringing in the laughs." Gene's recent attempts at voiceover work have all failed — he was set to voice one of the characters in *Over the Hedge* (2006) but didn't, and he was set to do a voiceover for a film called *Instant Karma*, a project that has now been canceled.

While Gene has turned down a number of films over the years, he never regretted any of his decisions, though there was one role he desperately wanted to play, that of a demented ventriloquist whose dummy speaks to him in the 1978 thriller *Magic*, a part that went to Anthony Hopkins. "The director [Richard Attenborough] wanted me, the writer [William Goldman] wanted me," Gene remembers. "[Producer] Joe Levine said, 'No, I don't want any comedians for this.' I'm not a comedian, but that's what it needed was someone who was trying to be funny but was really tragic."

Gene co-wrote a comedy with former *Cosby* writer and executive producer Tom Straw called *Cheek to Cheek*, about a recently released mental patient who thinks he's Fred Astaire and meets his own Ginger Rogers. Gene planned on starring in the film with Whoopi Goldberg but the film never got made. In 2005 Gene narrated the straight-to-video documentary *EXPO: Magic of the White City*, which told the story of 1893's Chicago World's Fair.

Since releasing his autobiography in March 2005, Gene has continued writing books, turning out one work of fiction almost every other year, all published by St. Martin's Press. In 2007 Gene's first novella, a seriocomic romance set during World War I provocatively titled *My French Whore*, was published. The film rights to *My French Whore* have been sold and Gene has written the screenplay, although he insists he will have no role as actor or producer. In 2008 Gene released his second novella, *The Woman Who Wouldn't*, about a troubled young violinist in 1903 who meets Anton Chekhov while at a health resort in Germany. In 2010 Gene published a collection of short stories entitled *What Is This Thing Called Love?* Three of the stories were about Gene's beloved late cousin Buddy, who spent his whole life looking for love but settled for sex. Gene uses his mother's maiden name for the last name of one of his protagonists. He also sets several of the stories in his hometown of Milwaukee and even includes his real-life friend Leonard Nimoy in one of the tales. As of this writing, he is working on his next book entitled *Humoresque*.

Though Gene has basically all but retired from acting, he said he would have liked to have found a project for him and Emma Thompson to do. "I admire her as an actress so much," he said. "I love her and I didn't know it until recently that her whole career started in comedy. And then she wrote me something, she said, 'If I had my druthers and we could start over again, you and I would do seventy-five comedies together.'" Thompson also confessed in a taped segment on the 74th Annual Academy Awards in which various stars talked about movies that influenced them, "I was really quite passionately in love for a long time with Gene Wilder in *Young Frankenstein*. I loved him and wanted to be his girlfriend."

On June 13, 2000, the American Film Institute announced their list of the 100 top film comedies of all time on a three-hour CBS special. AFI's 1,800-member jury composed of filmmakers, actors, critics, and historians listed four of Gene's films among the 100 best — *Blazing Saddles* (#6), *The Producers* (#11), *Young Frankenstein* (#13), and *Silver Streak* (#95). Cary Grant was the actor who appeared in the most films on the list (a total of eight), followed by the Marx Brothers and Woody Allen (five films each), while Gene joined Charlie Chaplin, Buster Keaton, Spencer Tracy, and Bill Murray as the only actors who each appeared in four films on the list.

On November 8, 2000, Gene was honored at the Second Annual International Jewish Film Festival. The two-week festival kicked off with a screening of *The Frisco Kid*. The screening and gala was held at the Academy of Motion Picture Arts and Sciences in Beverly Hills. The presentation was made by the festival's chairman, Arthur Hiller, and Gregory Peck, who had received the honor the previous year for his role in *Gentleman's Agreement* (1947).

"The award to Gene Wilder," said the festival's president and founder Phil Blazer, "is not only for his masterful work in this film classic about compassion and humor in Jewish life, but also for his continual efforts offscreen in support of so many humanitarian causes."

In 2001 Mel Brooks turned *The Producers* into a Broadway musical with — here's that name again — Nathan Lane playing Max Bialystock and Matthew Broderick as Leo Bloom. While it might have seemed impossible for Brooks to top his classic film, he did just that as *The Producers* became the hottest ticket in town, winning a record twelve Tony Awards and quickly becoming one of the biggest hits in Broadway history. Gene saw the show while it was in previews, but was noticeably absent from the star-studded opening night. "I didn't attend the premiere because I didn't want to take anything away from Matthew," he humbly explained. When Gene went backstage to meet the cast, Lane was so awestruck that, according to Gene, he "was close to tears. He said, 'If I knew you were coming I wouldn't have gone on today. I would have run away.'" As fond as Gene was of Zero Mostel, he gave Lane the ultimate compliment when he said, "I love Nathan in this so much. Nathan is funnier in this than Zero was."

In 2005 Brooks brought the musical version of *The Producers* to the big screen with Lane, Broderick, and most of the original stage cast reprising their roles. Unlike the Broadway show, the film was a critical and box-office flop.

In 2007 Brooks turned *Young Frankenstein* into a Broadway musical. It opened to mixed reviews and, despite running 485 performances, failed to become a blockbuster like *The Producers*, which ran for 2,502 performances. The show also drew criticism for Brooks' insistence on charging $450.00 for prime center orchestra seats, a greedy move worthy of Max Bialystock. "Mel was always driven by money," Gene said in a 2005 interview with Robert Chalmers of *The Independent*.

When Brooks told Gene he was bringing *Young Frankenstein* to the stage, Gene's first reaction was "over my dead body." The two had a very heated discussion over the phone, marking only the second time Gene and Brooks had fought during their friendship of more than forty years (the first disagreement occurring when Gene insisted Brooks have the "Puttin' on the Ritz" number in *Young Frankenstein*). A week later, Gene and Brooks spoke again, and this time Gene gave Brooks his blessing to go ahead with the musical of *Young Frankenstein*, partly because he felt bad for Brooks, who was still mourning Anne Bancroft, who died of uterine cancer at age 73 on June 6, 2005. "If I dampened that experience, I'd feel terrible for the rest of my life," Gene said. "I realised [sic] I had everything to win and nothing to lose. If it's a flop, they're not going to blame me, and if it's a success, everyone will remember this wonderful movie it's based on…I don't care. I just want him to be happy."

Sadly, Gene has seen a number of friends and colleagues die in recent years. Six months after Bancroft's death, Richard Pryor, who for years had suffered from multiple sclerosis, died of cardiac arrest at age 65; on December 12, 2006, Peter Boyle died of multiple myeloma and heart disease at age 71; on January 3, 2007, Chris Greenbury died of unknown causes at age 55; on June 29, 2007, Joel Siegel lost his battle with cancer at age 63; on August 12, 2007, Merv Griffin succumbed to prostate cancer at age 82; on May 4, 2009, Dom DeLuise died after a yearlong cancer struggle at age 75; on September 28, 2010, Arthur Penn died of congestive heart failure at age 88; and on November 5, 2010, Jill Clayburgh died of leukemia at age 66. Perhaps toughest for Gene, though, was the death of his cousin, Mark "Buddy" Silberman, whom Gene remained close with since the two were children (they were in the same graduating class at Washington High School). Buddy died of cardiac arrest on May 2, 2006 at age 73.

In 2001 the Las Vegas Film Critics Society's fifth annual Sierra Awards presented Gene with the William Holden Lifetime Achievement Award, an honor previously given to William Goldman, Jack Lemmon, Martin Scorsese, and Woody Allen.

In the summer of 2001, Gene returned to the stage yet again, this time at the Westport Country Playhouse. The show was called *Don't Make Me Laugh*, directed by Gene Saks and comprised of three short plays — *The Proposal* by Anton Chekhov, *The Music Cure* by George Bernard Shaw, and *Caught With His Trance Down* by Georges Feydeau. Gene adapted the Chekhov play and co-starred with Carol Kane and Bob Dishy. The show ran June 27–July 14, 2001, and, aside from his one-night-only performance of *Love Letters* in 1999, marked Gene's first American stage appearance in thirty-four years. The idea of doing the show developed after Joanne Woodward, who co-chairs the playhouse's artistic advisory council, invited Gene to be on the council.

In 2001 Gene and his brother-in-law Gil donated a number of scripts, papers, photos, and other memorabilia to the University of Iowa. The collection, known as The Gene Wilder Papers, includes materials from 1961–2000, with additional materials donated in 2001 and 2003 by Sharon R. Fox, who was active in his fan club.

Gene served as a consultant on a TV movie based on Gilda's autobiography that aired on ABC on April 29, 2002. *Gilda Radner: It's Always Something* starred Jami Gertz as Gilda and Tom Rooney as Gene. Gene gave his blessing to the project because of his long-standing friendship with Merv Griffin, whose company produced the film. Though Gene did not badmouth the film publicly, privately he thought it was a mess.

On November 7, 2002, Gene made a rare return to television in a guest appearance on the hit NBC series *Will & Grace*. In the episode, entitled "Boardroom and a Parked Place," Gene played Mr. Stein, the long-absent senior partner of the law firm where Will (Eric McCormack) works, who comes back after being in the London office. It turns out, however, that there is no London office — Stein actually had been away in a mental institution. Still unstable, he recruits Will to help him out with his cases and make important decisions, only to leave Will shunned by his co-workers, who feel he is kissing up to the boss. Gene reprised his role in a second episode of *Will & Grace* entitled "Sex, Losers & Videotape" that aired on April 3, 2003. In that episode, Mr. Stein, Will, and Karen (Megan Mullally) form a lonely hearts club, only for Stein and Karen to fall for one another, leaving Will all alone.

Gene's appearances on *Will & Grace* were so well-received that on September 13, 2003 he won an Emmy Award for Outstanding Guest Actor in a Comedy Series, beating out Hank Azaria (*Friends*), David Duchovny (*Life with Bonnie*), Fred Willard (*Everybody Loves Raymond*), and Jonathan Winters (*Life with Bonnie*). In a career that includes two Oscar and Golden Globe nominations, Gene's Emmy win marked his first major industry award at the age of seventy in the same category that earned Mel Brooks three consecutive Emmys for his guest appearances on *Mad About You* several years earlier. Gene did not show up to accept his award, which was presented during the technical Emmys a week before the prime-time broadcast. The winners in the guest acting categories are invited on the prime-time telecast as presenters, but Gene did not show up for that either.

On June 27, 2003, the day before what would have been Gilda's fifty-seventh birthday, the Hollywood Chamber of Commerce posthumously honored Gilda with a star on the Hollywood Walk of Fame at 6801 Hollywood Boulevard. While it would seem only natural for Gene to participate in the ceremony, he decided not to have any part of it. Gilda's brother Michael spoke on Gilda's behalf and was joined by comedians Molly Shannon, Fred Travalena, and Tom and Dick Smothers. Gilda's *Saturday Night Live* co-star Laraine Newman was also in attendance.

Out of respect for Karen, in recent years Gene has tried to distance himself from any tributes to Gilda. Another reason Gene did not attend the Hollywood Walk of Fame ceremony can be attributed to bad blood between him and Michael Radner, who Gene feels has taken advantage of and tried to profit from Gilda's name. Gene was particularly upset that Michael sold childhood home movies of Gilda to ABC for a tribute special that aired before the Gilda TV movie. In Michael Radner's defense, however, it should be noted that he had the same consultant role on the Gilda TV movie that Gene did, and was instrumental in putting together a two-disc tribute CD called *Voices for Gilda*, which was sold exclusively through Amazon.com and helped raise money for Gilda's Club. Gene did contribute to the CD, singing a very touching a cappella version of the song "Ohio" from the Leonard Bernstein musical *Wonderful Town*, a song he and Gilda used to entertain friends with at dinner parties. Gene was also absent when the corner of Sixth Avenue and West Houston Street, the block on which Gilda's Club is located in New York City, was renamed Gilda Radner Way in 2005. Joel Siegel, Paul Shaffer, Joanna Bull, and Alan Zweibel's wife Robin were there for the ceremony.

Gene serves on the board of directors of the Avon Theatre Film Center in Stamford, a movie house that first opened in 1939 and was restored in 2004 as an art house dedicated to showing classics, documentaries, and foreign films. Starting in 2007, Gene has been part of an annual three-night film series at the Avon called Wilder's Picks, in which he screens two of his favorite old films along with one of his own. The final showing of Gene's own film begins with a wine and cheese reception followed by a Q&A session with Gene that Karen moderates after the screening. Among the favorite films of Gene's that he has shown are *Random Harvest* (1942), *Key Largo* (1948), *Moulin Rouge* (1952), *Witness for the Prosecution* (1957), and *Soldier of Orange* (1979). *Young Frankenstein, The Adventure of Sherlock Holmes' Smarter Brother, The Frisco Kid,* and *The Woman in Red* are the films of Gene's that he has chosen to screen.

In 2008 Gene was scheduled to be transposed as a hologram of Jacob Marley's ghost in a stage production of *A Christmas Carol* at the Kodak Theatre in Los Angeles. The show used misleading ads that said "special appearance by Gene Wilder," failing to mention that Gene would not actually be appearing in person. At the last minute, they scrapped the hologram idea and hired an actual actor to play the role, disappointing many theatergoers who had purchased tickets thinking they would be seeing Gene live onstage.

When asked in the early 1970s who made him laugh, Gene cited Mel Brooks, Sid Caesar, Flip Wilson, Jonathan Winters, and *Sesame Street*. Some thirty years later, he told Larry King, "Dom DeLuise makes me laugh the most. If it's a good picture, Ben Stiller makes me laugh. Oddly enough, when I saw Robert DeNiro in *Meet the Parents* and *Analyze This*, Robert DeNiro made me laugh."

Despite Gene's insistence that he is not funny except in the movies, he seems to contradict himself whenever he says this in interviews by then muttering something that invariably gets a laugh from his interviewer, or in the case of when he was on *Inside the Actors Studio*, an entire audience. As soon as he walked on the stage, Gene shook hands with James Lipton and then proceeded to make sure his fly was zipped before sitting down. When Lipton asked Gene to talk about his childhood, Gene said, "Well…I was a happy-go-lucky guy till about…"The audience roared with laughter. Gene seemed stunned by the laughter and, almost as if apologizing, said, "I didn't mean for that to be funny."

If there are some actors who say funny things and others who say things funny, Gene Wilder clearly fits into the latter category. In fact, some of his best moments on-screen aren't necessarily lines of dialogue you could look at on paper and think would be all that amusing. But with a look in his eye or an expression or some business with his tongue, Gene can make the moment truly funny and truly his own.

Gene even has his own language of sorts for his more hyper moments, an odd mixture of baby talk, Jewish angst, and genuine fear that manifests itself in such nonsensical outbursts as in *Stir Crazy* when, after the judge sentences Gene and Richard Pryor to 125 years in prison, Gene screams out, "Wa! Wa! Wa!" Then there is his pseudo-Japanese gibberish when trying to pretend he's a karate master when he and Pryor first go to jail. In *Silver Streak* and *Hanky Panky*, Gene had moments when he was frightened flying in small planes, leading him to similar fits. This probably all started the moment Zero Mostel took away his little blue blanket in *The Producers*, and the ranting and raving hasn't stopped since.

Offscreen Gene Wilder may not always be "on" like Mel Brooks or Robin Williams, and now in his late seventies it doesn't seem likely that he will ever admit to being the life of the party, but after five decades in show business, he continues to realize the importance of laughter and has spoken about the effect his work can have on people. "I think the greatest thrill I have, of all the things that can happen to an actor," he said, "[is] when you meet someone who's been up the road and back and you see the pain in their eyes, and they grab your hand and say, 'I just want to say thank you 'cause I was in a lot of trouble, you know what I mean? I was in a lot of trouble. Everything's gone wrong. But I laughed. For two hours I laughed. God bless you for that.'"

Several of today's younger actors cite Gene Wilder as an influence, including Ben Stiller and Ryan Gosling, who called Gene "my Marlon Brando. I think he's one of the greatest actors of all time…"

Gene rarely goes to parties and has confessed that he prefers to have dinner with no more than three or four other people at a time ("More than six, I get nervous," he said). While a young actor in New York, Gene spent seven years in analysis, yet still admits, "I'm a dichotomy I don't quite understand. I'm soft-spoken but there's usually a volcano going on inside."

Gene has perhaps taken to heart his opening line from *Stir Crazy* in which he laments, "Who needs Hollywood? I hear they're really nuts out there." Though for years he divided his time between his homes in Bel Air and Stamford, Gene sold his California home in 2007 for $2.73 million. The 3-bedroom, 4 ½-bath Los Angeles ranch house at 10930 Chalon Road was built in 1951. Gene bought it in 1976 for $314,000. Gene now spends all of his time with Karen in the eighteenth-century Connecticut farmhouse on Scofieldtown Road that Gilda bought in 1981 and left to him in her will. Gene considers the 4-bedroom, 4-bath house, built in 1734 and surrounded by trees, "my greatest treasure, for the peace and tranquility that surrounds it." If Gene needs to stay in New York City overnight, his preference is the Carlyle Hotel on Madison Avenue and East 76th Street.

Aside from doctors' appointments and an occasional speaking engagement or book signing, Gene rarely leaves the house these days. There are exceptions, though. When Terence Marsh, one of Gene's closest friends, was honored with a lifetime achievement award from the Art Directors Guild on February 13, 2010, Gene flew to Los Angeles to present him the award. But usually when he sees friends or family, they visit him. Charles Grodin, who lives about twenty minutes from Gene in Wilton, Connecticut, usually stops by once a week, and Mel Brooks and Anne Bancroft were even known to stay the night, with Bancroft cooking dinner.

Gene remains very close to his sister Corinne and brother-in-law Gil (Corinne is the only person who still sometimes calls him Jerry). Corinne and Gil's son, Jordan Walker-Pearlman, has followed in Gene's filmmaking footsteps and works as an independent producer and director, most notably responsible for the 2000 prison drama *The Visit*. Gene has always been something of a mentor to Jordan, whom he regards as more like a son than a nephew.

To unwind, Gene likes reading, listening to classical music, playing bridge, watercolor painting (his self-portrait hangs above his living room fireplace), and watching old films on Turner Classic Movies with Karen. Gene has also caught up with the times and often spends hours on his computer surfing the Web and exchanging e-mails with various friends.

For most of his life, Gene looked younger than his age. His cancer treatments really took a toll on his appearance, though, and he no longer has the youthful exterior that most fans associate him with. Though the sparkling blue eyes remain the same, they are usually hidden behind glasses. Aside from no longer having the long curly locks he was so famous for, his face looks weathered and weary. He is only a few years shy of eighty and he looks it. At times he even appears frail, such as when he walked arm in arm with Alec Baldwin in a 2008 TCM special called *Role Model: Gene Wilder*, in which Baldwin, a huge fan of Gene's, interviewed him about his life and career.

While living in New York in the 1970s, Gene often bought his clothes at the high-end Bergdorf Goodman. Now, however, Gene dresses casually and rather dowdy, almost exclusively in blue. He is most comfortable in an old powder blue hooded sweatshirt — a "hoodie" as they're called today — which he usually wears at book signings. Otherwise, he can be seen in a sweater or turtleneck, both also in blue.

With Sparkle dead over a decade, in 2010 Gene adopted two small dogs, a Maltese and a Maltipoo. "When we got them, I figured they would either shorten my life or lengthen my life," he joked at a New York City book signing in April 2010. "I wasn't really sure which it would be. But now I think they are lengthening it, because we play together and have a lot of fun together."

Once one of the highest paid actors in film, Gene now leads a very quiet New England life, far from the glow of Hollywood that made him rich and famous over forty years ago. He spends most days in his study, a "haphazard but inviting room," according to Abigail Pogrebin, that boasts "an upright piano, a quilt draped over the piano seat, purplish wall-to-wall carpeting, a Macintosh computer on a wooden desk, videotapes on a shelf, and one or two of Wilder's own watercolors — surprisingly skilled — on the walls."

On his decision to no longer act unless something really special comes along, Gene says, "I'd rather write than act. Sit here in my comfortable study. Write. Come out for a cup of tea. Give my wife a kiss. Have a little yogurt. Come in and write some more."

As protective of his privacy as ever, Gene doesn't feel the need to attend movie premieres or awards shows. After five decades of laughter and twenty-two feature films (far too few for his most die-hard fans), Gene Wilder doesn't long for a star on the Hollywood

Walk of Fame or an Oscar or his name in the papers. When he says he is content just spending time with his wife painting watercolors, he's not trying to be humble — he means it. "I am in love," he told Robert Chalmers in 2005. "With my wife. This is the only... great love that I have experienced ever, in my life. And this is the other thing that I have learnt from cancer: that the greatest joy on earth is to love and to be loved. And I have that. I am surrounded by birds, and flowers, and trees...And deer. I live where I want to live. With the person I want to be with. And for me...that is more than enough."

# Acknowledgments

The author wishes to express his gratitude to the following individuals who have helped make this book possible. For their openness and generosity in granting me interviews, sincere thanks to Arthur Hiller, Earl Hurwitz, Kelly LeBrock, Mace Neufeld, Fred Schuler, David Steinberg, Norman Steinberg, Mel Stuart, and Bud Yorkin.

Lois J. Molitor's detective work would make even Sherlock Holmes jealous (let alone any younger brothers he may have had) and I am grateful for her help in locating crucial documents regarding Gene Wilder's family history. I can think of no way to sufficiently thank John A. Simone Jr. for sharing some incredibly useful information with me and for giving me and this book numerous mentions on the Gene Wilder tribute Web site he used to operate. Additional thanks to Dr. Eleanor Haille, Darryl Wrobel, and Jarrod LaBine.

The publishing world would be a nicer place if there were more people like Ben Ohmart, who saw the merits of publishing this book when literally hundreds of others passed on it. Thanks also to Ben's crackerjack editing and design team of Sandra Grabman and Brian Pearce for their help and almost saintly patience.

Thank you to Frank Sanello for trying to help a first-time author get a break, Stephen Wetta for encouragement early on, James

Tomkins for suggesting I bring this book to BearManor, and the late Billy Puzo, a great friend and artist who always had faith in me.

I also want to thank every writer, journalist, and interviewer whose source material I drew from. I could not have written this biography without their wonderful books, articles, and profiles.

Most of all, though, thank you to my parents, Martin and Bella Mednick, whose love and support make everything I do possible.

# Notes

## 1. WISCONSIN: WHERE THE CHEESE COMES FROM

13: "My name was Jerry Silberman" — *Great Romances of the Twentieth Century: Gene Wilder & Gilda Radner*, Women's Entertainment Network, January 14, 2002.

15: "If I start out as Jerry Silberman" — *Extreme Close-Up*, E! Entertainment Television, July 26, 1991.

15: "They started tossing out names" — Ibid.

16: "I had always liked Gene" — Leo Seligsohn, "On the Wilder Side," *Newsday*, December 18, 1977.

16: "Did you ever stop" — *Extreme Close-Up*.

16: "I thought it had a good sound" — Seligsohn, "On the Wilder Side."

17: "very innocent, very naive" — *Bravo Profiles: Gene Wilder*, Bravo, December 5, 2001.

17: "very artistic, temperamental" — Ibid.

17: "The doctor" — Ibid.

17: "The first one was" — *Extreme Close-Up*.

17: "I knew I scored" — Ibid.

18: "I'll now give my" — Ibid.

18: "I supposed I tried" — Ibid.

18: "It was not pleasant" — *The Dick Cavett Show*, CNBC, July 27, 1991.

18: "I couldn't bring myself" — Merv Griffin with Peter Barsocchini, *Merv Griffin's Book of People* (New York: Arbor House, 1982), pp. 67-68.

19: "I wanted to be" — *Inside the Actors Studio*, Bravo, September 25, 1996.

19: "I saw a great" — Patricia Nolan, "The Way They Were — Gene Wilder," *Rona Barrett's Hollywood*, May 1977.

19: "I even got to the point" — Ibid.

19: "heart would pound if" — Seligsohn, "On the Wilder Side."

20: "I was sexually embarrassed" — Craig Modderno, "Gene Wilder: I Thrive on Embarrassment!" *Rona Barrett's Hollywood*, July 1976.

20: "Something went wrong" — *Entertainment Tonight*, July 26, 1986.

21: "they were teaching all" — *New York Sunday News*, August 16, 1970.

21: "I should have been a patient" — E! Entertainment Television, July 26, 1991.

21: "The one thing it did" — Ibid.

21: "[My dad and I] were walking" — *Bravo Profiles*.

22: "There was this funny-looking boy" — Charles Grodin, *It Would Be So Nice If You Weren't Here: My Journey Through Show Business* (New York: Morrow, 1989), p. 74.

## 2. A CAREER IN BLOOM

25: "I don't mind talking personal" — *Entertainment Tonight*, July 26, 1986.

25: "When it comes time" — Ibid.

26: "Put me on *The Tonight Show*" — *Later with Bob Costas*, NBC, May 3, 1989.

26: "Gene was already" — Author's interview with David Steinberg, September 25, 2010.

26: "I hope I didn't do anything" — Ibid.

26: "To be on with" — Judy Nathanson and Diane McDonald, eds., *Geneology: The Gene Wilder Fan Club Journal*, Fall 1979.

27: "dredged up some" — Author's phone conversation with Mary Mercier, April 10, 1996.

27: "She's a very nice lady" — Jacqui Nicholson, "Gene Wilder — The 'Funny Man' Who Hides Nothing," *Rona Barrett's Hollywood*, June 1975.

27: "traumatic" — Leo Seligsohn, "On the Wilder Side," *Newsday*, December 18, 1977.

27: "I fell in love in Paris" — Ibid.

28: "I thought I was in love" — Catherine Deveney, "Wackier, weirder, Wilder," *Scotland on Sunday*, May 20, 2007.

28: "I thought they got along" — Author's interview with Bud Yorkin, April 9, 1996.

28: "When we weren't working" — Barbara Bauer, "Gene Wilder — manic to romantic," *Bijou*, June 1977.

28: "She started representing me" — Ibid.

29: "He had written" — *Later with Bob Costas*.

30: "There was a numbness" — Kirk Douglas, *The Ragman's Son* (New York: Simon and Schuster, 1988), p. 366.

30: "I can't stand screamers" — Ralph Appelbaum, "Reality...the artist and the Romantic Clown," *Films*, July 1981.

30: "There's a man named Charles Grodin" — Charles Grodin, *It Would Be So Nice If You Weren't Here: My Journey Through Show Business* (New York: Morrow, 1989), p. 154.

31: "I had to start out" — *The Dick Cavett Show*, CNBC, July 27, 1991.

32: "I didn't hear from him" — *Later with Bob Costas*.

32: "The only thing is" — Jared Brown, *Zero Mostel* (New York: Atheneum, 1989), p. 264.

32: "My heart was pounding" — Ibid., p. 264.

33: "Joseph E. Levine" — *Inside the Actors Studio*, Bravo, September 25, 1996.

33: "It was right out" — Jason E. Squire, ed., *The Movie Business Book*, 2nd ed. (New York: Fireside, 1992), p. 58.

35: "You may have heard" — Brown, *Zero Mostel*, p. 265.

35: "It wasn't a consuming passion" — Ibid., p. 265.

35: "mellowed" — Ibid., p. 121.

36: "I was just praying" — *Larry King Live*, CNN, May 2, 2002.

36: "would have been" — *Bravo Profiles: Gene Wilder*, Bravo, December 5, 2001.

## 3. YOU SAY YOU WANT A REVOLUTION

37: "dueling competition" — Mason Wiley and Damien Bona, *Inside Oscar: The Unofficial History of the Academy Awards* (New York: Ballantine Books, 1986), p. 421.

38: "Everybody was stunned" — Author's interview with Bud Yorkin, April 9, 1996.

38: "It didn't make a lot of money" — Ibid.

39: "What's really interesting" — Ibid.

## 4. THE LUCK OF THE IRISH

42: "I just roamed around" — *New York Sunday News*, August 16, 1970.

## 5. CHOCOLATE AND SEX

44: "I said" — Author's interview with Mel Stuart, April 24, 1996.

44: "Dave, this is Willy Wonka" — Ibid.

45: "You've got it" — Ibid.

45: "I would like to come out" — *Inside the Actors Studio*, Bravo, September 25, 1996.

45: "brilliant idea" — *Bravo Profiles: Gene Wilder*, Bravo, December 5, 2001.

46: "I was making an adult picture" — Stuart interview.

47: "He took the book" — Ibid.

47: "He knew the kid" — Ibid.

47: "My God" — Ibid.

47: "I don't care" — Ibid.

48: "I got a set here" — Ibid.

48: "Brilliant fairy tale ending line" — Ibid.

48: "Everybody thought" — Ibid.

49: "It's no mystery" — Ibid.

49: "was a maniac" — Judy Nathanson and Christine Gardener, eds., *Geneology: The Gene Wilder Fan Club Journal*, Spring 1977.

49: "He really thought that out" — Stuart interview.

49: "I have found" — Ibid.

50: "It was a film" — Nathanson and Gardener, *Geneology*.

50: "I don't want my gravestone" — Amy Kover, "Pure Imagination," *TV Guide*, January 26, 2002.

50: "all about money" — Michael Shelden, "Why would they remake Willy Wonka?" *The Daily Telegraph*, June 1, 2005.

50: "I like Johnny Depp" — Ibid.

51: "But instead of Jennifer Jones" — *Later with Bob Costas*, NBC, May 3, 1989.

52: "I did like that sheep" — Ibid.

52: "Woody is one of the nicest people" — Patricia Nolan, "The Way They Were — Gene Wilder," *Rona Barrett's Hollywood*, May 1977.

52: "Working with Woody" — Kenneth Tynan, "Frolics and Detours of a Short Hebrew Man," *The New Yorker*, October 30, 1978.

## 6. A VERY GOOD YEAR

56: "not to do or say much" — Jared Brown, *Zero Mostel* (New York: Atheneum, 1989), p. 282.

56: "there was never a producer" — Ibid., p. 282.

56: "did not really understand" — Ibid., p. 282.

57: "It was a bad film" — Ibid., p. 283.

57: "One of the best things" — Judy Nathanson and Diane McDonald, eds., *Geneology: The Gene Wilder Fan Club Journal*, Spring 1977.

58: "You would be great" — Author's interview with Norman Steinberg, August 12, 1998.

59: "He saved my life" — Mel Brooks director commentary, *Young Frankenstein* DVD, Twentieth Century Fox Home Entertainment.

59: "Gene did not look" — *Bravo Profiles: Gene Wilder*, Bravo, December 5, 2001.

59: "I knew *Blazing Saddles*" — Richard Pryor, *Pryor Convictions and Other Life Sentences* (New York: Pantheon Books, 1995), pp. 132-33.

61: "One afternoon" — Leo Seligsohn, "On the Wilder Side," *Newsday*, December 18, 1977.

61: "I called Mel" — Barbara Hoffman, "Still a scream — and back on screen," *New York Post*, August 8, 1999.

61: "How about we make a picture" — Ibid.

62: "You're whistling 'Dixie'" — *Larry King Live*, CNN, May 2, 2002.

62: "What are you getting me into?" — Ibid.

63: "I was close to rage" — *Making Frankensense of Young Frankenstein* (1996), *Young Frankenstein* DVD, Twentieth Century Fox Home Entertainment.

63: "You're timid and you're shy" — *Bravo Profiles.*

64: "the happiest film experience" — Hoffman, "Still a scream."

65: "I was terribly sad" — Ibid.

65: "Gene, what is it?" — Ibid.

65: "Madeline is not now" — Craig Modderno, "Gene Wilder: I Thrive on Embarrassment!" *Rona Barrett's Hollywood,* July 1976.

65: "She was fresh and funny" — Mel Brooks director commentary.

65: "good pals" — Modderno, "I Thrive on Embarrassment!"

## 7. AUTEUR! AUTEUR!

67: "I love directing" — Ralph Appelbaum, "Reality...the artist and the Romantic Clown," *Films,* July 1981.

69: "After the picture was shot" — Leo Seligsohn, "On the Wilder Side," *Newsday,* December 18, 1977.

70: "If he ever worked with me" — Jay Samuels, "Gene Wilder: Out of sadness — comedy," *Courier-Post* (Cherry Hill, NJ), January 3, 1977.

70: "It was put together" — Charles Moritz, ed., *Current Biography Yearbook 1977* (New York: The H.W. Wilson Company, 1977), p. 242.

72: "the group that" — Jeff Rovin, "First Films," *Video Movies,* April 1984.

73: "all subjective" — The Movie Channel, 1987.

73: "don't know anything" — Ibid.

73: "There are very few critics" — Robert Barrett, "Making Laughs at Nogales Airport," *The Arizona Republic,* January 21, 1979.

73: "I know at this point" — *Entertainment Tonight,* July 26, 1986.

## 8. A WINNING STREAK

76: "He said" — Author's interview with Arthur Hiller, August 13, 1998.

76: "It was the best film script" — Judy Nathanson and Christine Gardener, eds., *Geneology: The Gene Wilder Fan Club Journal*, Spring 1977.

76: "Another studio" — Bob Thomas, "Comeback Of Gene Wilder," *Los Angeles Herald-Examiner*, May 13, 1976.

77: "We were worried" — Roger Ebert, "Hanging out with Wilder and Pryor," *Chicago Sun-Times*, December 23, 1976.

78: "in the course of filming" — Jim Haskins, *Richard Pryor: A Man and His Madness* (New York: Beaufort Books, 1984), p. 104.

78: "In box office terms" — Hiller interview.

79: "She's a misfit" — "Wilder ecstatic about 'ideal wife' Carol Kane," *Valley News & Greensheet*, July 1977.

79: "It was Christmas time" — Leo Seligsohn, "On the Wilder Side," *Newsday*, December 18, 1977.

80: "greatest influence" — "*Gallery* Interview: Gene Wilder," *Gallery*, June 1981.

80: "I don't want to produce anymore" — Robert Barrett, "Making Laughs at Nogales Airport," *The Arizona Republic*, January 21, 1979.

## 9. A KOSHER COWBOY

85: "I can't do this" — Mel Brooks director commentary, *Blazing Saddles* DVD, Warner Home Video.

86: "Gene was an absolute perfect ten" — Author's interview with Mace Neufeld, June 1, 1999.

87: "[A]t one point" — Abigail Pogrebin, *Stars of David: Prominent Jews Talk About Being Jewish* (New York: Broadway Books, 2005), p. 97.

87: "Gene is brilliant" — Garry Jenkins, *Harrison Ford: Imperfect Hero* (Secaucus: Birch Lane Press, 1998), p. 147.

87: "Even though" — Neufeld interview.

## 10. "THAT'S RIGHT! WE BAAAAD!"

90: "I understand...taken hostage" — Jim Haskins, *Richard Pryor: A Man and His Madness* (New York: Beaufort Books, 1984), p. 183.

90: "There's a little scene" — Ralph Appelbaum, "Reality...the artist and the Romantic Clown," *Films*, July 1981.

91: "ramshackle home" — Richard Pryor, *Pryor Convictions and Other Life Sentences* (New York: Pantheon Books, 1995), p. 182.

91: "Gene is a very respectful person" — Author's interview with Fred Schuler, August 31, 1998.

93: "tastefully, semi-pornographic love story" — Appelbaum, "Reality."

## 11. THIS NICE JEWISH GIRL FROM DETROIT

95: "I've been married twice" — Ralph Appelbaum, "Reality...the artist and the Romantic Clown," *Films*, July 1981.

97: "I'd give it all up for love" — Diane Rosen, "Gilda!" *TV Guide*, July 29, 1978.

97: "funny and athletic" — Gilda Radner, *It's Always Something* (New York: Simon and Schuster, 1989), p.15.

97: "A funny man" — *Entertainment Tonight*, July 26, 1986.

97: "I thought this...bitch" — *PM Magazine*, July 22, 1986.

98: "She thought I was queer" — Ibid.

98: "After seeing his movies" — Ibid.

98: "She had seen my movies" — Michael J. Bandler, "Gene Wilder," *US*, May 29, 1989.

99: "If I made one mistake" — *Extreme Close-Up*, E! Entertainment Television, July 26, 1991.

99: "learned it could be a pleasure" — Radner, *It's Always Something*, p. 18.

99: "Gene said he was suffocating" — Ibid., p. 19.

100: "Gene built a tennis court" — David Saltman, *Gilda: An Intimate Portrait* (Chicago: Contemporary Books, 1992), p. 226.

100: "My new 'career'" — Radner, *It's Always Something*, p. 16.

100: "He believed that he" — Author's interview with Fred Schuler, August 31, 1998.

101: "Gene was wonderful" — Author's interview with Kelly LeBrock, November 9, 1998.

103: "She was very insecure" — *Face to Face with Connie Chung*, CBS, May 7, 1990.

103: "I know you love me" — Ibid.

103: "I'd been waiting" — Ibid.

103: "Why didn't you marry" — Radner, *It's Always Something*, p. 28.

## 12. WHERE WOLF?

106: "*Haunted Honeymoon* was probably" — Author's interview with
    Fred Schuler, August 31, 1998.
106: "I think his strength" — Ibid.
107: "I don't know if it was" — *Bravo Profiles: Gene Wilder*, Bravo,
    December 5, 2001.

## 13. IN SICKNESS AND IN HEALTH

110: "probably influenced" — Gilda Radner, *It's Always Something*
    (New York: Simon and Schuster, 1989), p. 32.
110: "fog rolling in" — Ibid., p. 48.
111: "made jokes about cancer" — M. Steven Piver, M.D. with Gene
    Wilder, *Gilda's Disease* (New York: Prometheus, 1996), p. 31.

## 14. ROAD TO WELLNESS

113: "it was as though an angel" — Gilda Radner, *It's Always Something*
    (New York: Simon and Schuster, 1989), p. 80.
114: "The last place I thought" — Pat Dougherty, "Gilda," *Life*, March
    1988.
114: "It's not voo-doo" — Ibid.
115: "I had wanted" — Radner, *It's Always Something*, p. 268.

## 15. COLOR BLIND MOVIE MAGIC

117: "I know it's hard" — Martin Kasindorf, "Two for the Show,"
    *Newsday*, May 7, 1989.
117: "he feared being" — Frank Sanello, *Eddie Murphy: The Life and
    Times of a Comic on the Edge* (New York: Birch Lane Press, 1997),
    p. 60.
118: "lacked something" — Author's interview with Arthur Hiller,
    August 13, 1998.
118: "It didn't ring true" — Kasindorf, "Two for the Show."
118: "No hard feelings" — Ibid.
118: "I said, boy" — Hiller interview.

119: "I wanted to make sure" — *Good Morning America*, ABC, November 7, 1988.

119: "They use our disability" — *Entertainment Tonight*, June 2, 1989.

119: "We wanted to make sure" — Ibid.

119: "There were communication tips" — Ibid.

119: "So I said" — *Behind the Scenes*, HBO, April 1990.

119: "You wonder" — *Good Morning America*, ABC, May 12, 1989.

120: "We don't know" — *Good Morning America*, ABC, May 9, 1989.

120: "We have almost" — *Good Morning America*, ABC, November 7, 1988.

120: "They are both actors" — Hiller interview.

120: "lackluster" — Richard Pryor, *Pryor Convictions and Other Life Sentences* (New York: Pantheon Books, 1995), p. 227.

121: "My excuse was the money" — Ibid., p. 227.

## 16. THE DAY THE LAUGHTER DIED

123: "Gilda was so sick" — Author's interview with Arthur Hiller, August 13, 1998.

124: "I was so incredibly dumb" — *Larry King Live*, CNN, May 2, 2002.

124: "She'd pull herself" — Ibid.

124: "Great" — *Later with Bob Costas*, NBC, May 3, 1989.

124: "Oh, God" — Susan Schindehette, "Saturday Night Sweetheart," *People*, June 5, 1989.

124: "the people there" — Jane Sims Podesta, "Why Did Gilda Die?" *People*, June 3, 1991.

124: "Come on" — Ibid.

124: "She looked like an angel" — Ibid.

124: "While she was conscious" — Ibid.

125: "It was a beautiful ceremony" — *Gilda Radner: The E! True Hollywood Story*, E! Entertainment Television, October 19, 1997.

125: "I only had one great thing" — *Face to Face with Connie Chung*, CBS, May 7, 1990.

126: "If she had been" — Ibid.

126: "People write to me" — Ibid.

126: "At first I didn't think" — Podesta, "Why Did Gilda Die?"

127: "A certain part" — *Face to Face.*

## 17. BACK TO WORK

129: "I read it and I thought" — *Good Morning America*, ABC, September 21, 1990.
130: "He was pretty raw" — *Good Morning America*, ABC, September 20, 1990.
130: "I don't think" — *Good Morning America*, ABC, September 21, 1990.
132: "I was bitterly disappointed" — Author's interview with Norman Steinberg, August 12, 1998.
132: "maybe the best actress" — *Good Morning America*, ABC, September 21, 1990.
132: "In my opinion" — HBO Entertainment News, September 1990.
132: "I should've been funnier" — *Inside the Actors Studio*, Bravo, September 25, 1996.

## 18. NOT ANOTHER HIT

157: "If we would see each other" — *Showbiz Today*, CNN, July 25, 1991.

## 19. IN LOVE AGAIN

159: "I'm not going to retire" — *Extreme Close-Up*, E! Entertainment Television, July 26, 1991.
161: "But it's quarter to eight" — *The Insider*, March 15, 2005.
162: "the best years of my life" — *Face to Face with Connie Chung*, CBS, May 7, 1990.
162: "I didn't even see them" — Author's interview with Arthur Hiller, August 13, 1998.
163: "Pretty soon" — Diane Clehane, "Wilder at Heart," *TV Guide*, November 18, 2000.
163: "If someone dies" — *Extreme Close-Up*.
164: "the most intuitive" — *Good Morning America*, ABC, July 22, 1991.
164: "She is the great love" — Clehane, "Wilder at Heart."
164: "I was very unhappy" — *InnerVIEWS with Ernie Manouse*, March 9, 2007.

## 20. WELCOME TO THE CLUB

165: "With all the great" — Pat Dougherty, "Gilda," *Life*, March 1988.

167: "Medical science" — Gilda's Club promotional video, 1994.

168: "We see Gilda's Club" — Ibid.

168: "One of the first" — Ibid.

168: "We're calling it" — Ibid.

168: "I don't think she'd say" — Diane Clehane, "Wilder at Heart," *TV Guide*, November 18, 2000.

169: "I was...Mr. Cancer" — Ibid.

## 21. NOT READY FOR PRIME TIME

171: "I've contemplated" — Robert Barrett, "Making Laughs at Nogales Airport," *The Arizona Republic*, January 21, 1979.

175: "The series is a chance" — "Anything for a Gag," *TV Guide*, December 17, 1994.

177: "I'm asked to do theatre" — Matt Wolf, "Gene Wilder makes some funny choices," Associated Press, November 6, 1996.

## 22. SUCH A NICE JEWISH DETECTIVE

179: "You can't be a television actor" — Robert Barrett, "Making Laughs at Nogales Airport," *The Arizona Republic*, January 21, 1979.

181: "Someone at A&E" — A&E promotional materials.

181: "My wife" — Ibid.

182: "There had always been" — Ibid.

183: "There are more authentic" — John Sellers, "Getting Away with Murder," *TV Guide*, January 9, 1999.

183: "I don't want to make" — A&E.

183: "I was surprised" — Ibid.

184: "high ratings" — John Dempsey, "A&E's Wolfe pack: net preps new mystery pic," *Daily Variety*, January 15, 1999.

184: "Everything I do" — Richard Huff, "'Alice' Glitters with Stars," New York *Daily News*, February 28, 1999.

185: "Everything I did" — Ibid.

187: "I guess" — James O'Keefe, "Wilder to return to stage in
    Westport," *The Stamford Advocate*, May 4, 2001.

## 23. A PRIVATE BATTLE

191: "There's an enormous" — Richard Johnson and Cathy Burke,
    "Wilder 'in remission'," *New York Post*, February 5, 2000.
192: "lymphoma is one" — Ibid.
192: "a real health nut" — "A Quiet Battle," *People*, February 21, 2000
192: "You want her" — Ibid.
192: "very positive and smart" — Ibid.
192: "This drug" — "A Brighter Outlook for Lymphoma Patients,"
    New York *Daily News*, February 7, 2000.
193: "He said he really liked" — Author's e-mail exchange with Bonnie
    Hunter.
193: "really bad" — Martin Gould and Stephanie Timm, "Gene Wilder
    Battling Cancer," *Star*, February 15, 2000.
193: "His face was puffy" — Ibid.
193: "I wouldn't say" — Hunter e-mail.
193: "His hair was quite longer too" — Ibid.
194: "He's out of the hospital" — Author's conversation with Susan
    Ruskin, March 8, 2000.
194: "Nathan Lane's co-star" — Richard Johnson, *New York Post*,
    September 15, 2000.
194: "lucky ones" — Gene Wilder, *Kiss Me Like a Stranger: My Search
    for Love and Art* (New York: St. Martin's Press, 2005), p. 249.
194: "Things can happen" — Diane Clehane, "Wilder at Heart," *TV
    Guide*, November 18, 2000.
194: "When I was a kid" — *Bravo Profiles: Gene Wilder*, Bravo,
    December 5, 2001.

## 24. GOD AND POLITICS

195: "I'm quietly political" — "Gene Wilder Is Rooting For The
    Democrats," Starpulse News Blog, *www.starpulse.com*, May 15,
    2007.

197: "I don't think...stupid" — Tom Gogola, "When Wilder Was the World," *Fairfield Weekly*, November 16, 2006.

198: "I like Barack Obama" — "Rooting For The Democrats."

198: "I saw Christopher Reeve" — Ibid.

198: "Not being Catholic" — *Extreme Close-Up*, E! Entertainment Television, July 26, 1991.

198: "You asked Stephen Hawking" — *Larry King Live*, CNN, May 2, 2002.

198: "Gene, if heaven exists" — *Inside the Actors Studio*, Bravo, September 25, 1996.

198: "Well, I think that heaven" — Ibid.

199: "Hi, honey" — Ibid.

199: "For example" — Ralph Appelbaum, "Reality...the artist and the Romantic Clown," *Films*, July 1981.

199: "I married a Catholic" — Abigail Pogrebin, *Stars of David: Prominent Jews Talk About Being Jewish* (New York: Broadway Books, 2005), p. 97.

199: "When I was" — Appelbaum, "Reality."

199: "I'm going to tell you" — Pogrebin, *Stars of David*, p. 93.

## 25. CONNECTICUT: PEACE AND TRANQUILITY

201: "I don't like show business" — "Gene Wilder Is Still Waiting For Golden Ticket," Starpulse News Blog, *www.starpulse.com*, May 16, 2007.

203: "It overwhelms me" — Craig Modderno, "Gene Wilder: I Thrive on Embarrassment!" *Rona Barrett's Hollywood*, July 1976.

203: "Arkin and Hoffman" — Jacqui Nicholson, "Gene Wilder — The 'Funny Man' Who Hides Nothing," *Rona Barrett's Hollywood*, June 1975.

204: "His face looks like" — Vincent Canby, "'Greatest Lover,' Great Comedy," *The New York Times*, December 19, 1977.

204: "He hasn't become" — Barbara Bauer, "Gene Wilder: manic to romantic," *Bijou*, June 1977.

204: "handsome" — Patricia Nolan, "The Way They Were — Gene Wilder," *Rona Barrett's Hollywood*, May 1977.

204: "ugly-handsome" — Nicholson, "Hides Nothing."

204: "a latter-day Harp Marx" — Tom Shales, "Fall TV Preview; A Dip in the Gene Pool; NBC's Refreshing 'Something Wilder'," *The Washington Post*, October 1, 1994.

204: "a male…Shirley Temple" — Jeff Jarvis, *TV Guide*, February 4, 1995.

204: "When I was a little boy" — Judy Nathanson and Christine Gardener, eds., *Geneology: The Gene Wilder Fan Club Journal*, Spring 1977.

204: "wispy" — Bruce Weber, "Courtship Follies From Chekhov, Shaw and Feydeau," *The New York Times*, July 6, 2001.

204: "I have found" — Author's e-mail exchange with John A. Simone Jr.

204: "America's Peter Sellers" — Bauer, "manic to romantic."

205: "seems an inspired original" — Pauline Kael, "A Magnetic Blur," *The New Yorker*, December 30, 1974.

205: "I stepped out" — Matt Wolf, "Gene Wilder makes some funny choices," Associated Press, November 6, 1996.

205: "I was not fat" — Michael J. Bandler, "Gene Wilder," *US*, May 29, 1989.

205: "When he's at home" — Debbi Pascua, *Geneology: The Gene Wilder Fan Club Journal*, Fall 1978.

205: "We share" — *The Martha Stewart Show*, NBC Universal Television Distribution, April 16, 2007.

207: "The director…wanted me" — *Larry King Live*, CNN, May 2, 2002.

208: "I admire her" — Ibid.

208: "I was…passionately in love" — 74th Annual Academy Awards, ABC, March 24, 2002.

208: "The award to Gene Wilder" — Second Annual International Jewish Film Festival press release, July 13, 2000.

209: "I didn't attend" — Tom DiNardo, "Gene Wilder: I've Won My Battle With Cancer," *National Enquirer*, May 22, 2001.

209: "was close to tears" — *Broadway Premieres The Producers*, UPN 9 News, April 22, 2001.

209: "I love Nathan" — Ibid.

209: "Mel was always driven" — Robert Chalmers, "Gene Wilder: An Angel In America," *The Independent*, June 19, 2005.

209: "over my dead body" — Susan Dominus, "I like show but I don't like the business," *The Daily Telegraph*, April 22, 2007.

209: "If I dampened" — Ibid.

213: "Dom DeLuise makes me laugh" — *Larry King Live*.

213: "Well... I was" — *Inside the Actors Studio*, Bravo, September 25, 1996.

214: "I think the greatest thrill" — *Extreme Close-Up*, E! Entertainment Television, July 26, 1991.

214: "my Marlon Brando" — Edward Douglas, "Ryan Gosling Ain't No Dummy!" *www.comingsoon.net*, October 15, 2007.

214: "More than six" — *Extreme Close-Up*.

214: "I'm a dichotomy" — Ibid.

216: "When we got them" — Dorothy Cascerceri, "New Leash on Life for Gene Wilder," *National Enquirer*, May 24, 2010.

216: "haphazard but inviting room" — Abigail Pogrebin, *Stars of David: Prominent Jews Talk About Being Jewish* (New York: Broadway Books, 2005), p. 93.

216: "I'd rather write than act" — Dominus, "I like show."

217: "I am in love" — Chalmers, "Angel In America."

# Bibliography

"Anything for a Gag." *TV Guide*, December 17, 1994.

Appelbaum, Ralph. "Reality...the artist and the Romantic Clown." *Films*, July 1981.

Bandler, Michael J. "Gene Wilder." *US*, May 29, 1989.

Barrett, Robert. "Making Laughs at Nogales Airport." *The Arizona Republic*, January 21, 1979.

Bauer, Barbara. "Gene Wilder: manic to romantic." *Bijou*, June 1977.

Beck, Marilyn, and Stacy Jenel Smith. "Mind-boggling surprises fill Prinze flick." New York *Daily News*, April 14, 1999.

Bianco, Robert. "Nice 'Lady'." *USA Today*, December 10, 1999.

"A Brighter Outlook for Lymphoma Patients." New York *Daily News*, February 7, 2000.

Brown, Dennis. *Shop Talk*. New York: Newmarket Press, 1992.

Brown, Jared. *Zero Mostel*. New York: Atheneum, 1989.

Canby, Vincent. "'Greatest Lover,' Great Comedy." *The New York Times*, December 19, 1977.

Cascerceri, Dorothy. "New Leash on Life for Gene Wilder." *National Enquirer*, May 24, 2010.

Chalmers, Robert. "Gene Wilder: An Angel In America." *The Independent*, June 19, 2005.

Clehane, Diane. "Wilder at Heart." *TV Guide*, November 18, 2000.

Dahl, Roald. *Charlie and the Chocolate Factory*. New York: Alfred A. Knopf, Inc., 1964.

Dempsey, John. "A&E's Wolfe pack: net preps new mystery pic." *Daily Variety*, January 15, 1999.

Deveney, Catherine. "Wackier, weirder, Wilder." *Scotland on Sunday*, May 20, 2007.

DiNardo, Tom. "Gene Wilder: I've Won My Battle With Cancer." *National Enquirer*, May 22, 2001.

Dominus, Susan. "I like show but I don't like the business." *The Daily Telegraph*, April 22, 2007.

Dougherty, Pat. "Gilda." *Life*, March 1988.

Douglas, Edward. "Ryan Gosling Ain't No Dummy!" *www.comingsoon.net*, October 15, 2007.

Douglas, Kirk. *The Ragman's Son*. New York: Simon and Schuster, 1988.

Ebert, Roger. "Hanging out with Wilder and Pryor." *Chicago Sun-Times*, December 23, 1976.

— . *Roger Ebert's Movie Home Companion 1987 Edition*. Kansas City: Andrews, McMeel & Parker, 1986.

Fung, Lisa. "Jane Seymour drops out of 'A Christmas Carol' at the Kodak Theatre." *Los Angeles Times*, December 22, 2008.

"*Gallery* Interview: Gene Wilder." *Gallery*, June 1981.

"Gene Wilder Is Rooting For The Democrats." Starpulse News Blog, *www.starpulse.com*, May 15, 2007.

"Gene Wilder Is Still Waiting For Golden Ticket." Starpulse News Blog, *www.starpulse.com*, May 16, 2007.

Gogola, Tom. "When Wilder Was the World." *Fairfield Weekly*, November 16, 2006.

Gould, Martin, and Stephanie Timm. "Gene Wilder Battling Cancer." *Star*, February 15, 2000.

Griffin, Merv, with Peter Barsocchini. *Merv Griffin's Book of People*. New York: Arbor House, 1982.

Grodin, Charles. *It Would Be So Nice If Your Weren't Here: My Journey Through Show Business*. New York: Morrow, 1989.

Haskins, Jim. *Richard Pryor: A Man and His Madness*. New York: Beaufort Books, 1984.

Hoffman, Barbara. "Still a scream — and back onscreen." *New York Post*, August 8, 1999.

Huff, Richard. " 'Alice' Glitters with Stars." New York *Daily News*, February 28, 1999.

Jarvis, Jeff. *TV Guide*, February 4, 1995.

Jenkins, Garry. *Harrison Ford: Imperfect Hero*. Secaucus: Birch Lane Press, 1998.

Johnson, Richard, and Cathy Burke. "Wilder 'in remission.'" *New York Post*, February 5, 2000.

Johnson, Richard. *New York Post*, September 15, 2000.

Kael, Pauline. "A Magnetic Blur." *The New Yorker*, December 30, 1974.

Kasindorf, Martin. "Two for the Show." *Newsday*, May 7, 1989.

Kover, Amy. "Pure Imagination." *TV Guide*, January 26, 2002.

Littleton, Cynthia. "Autobiography basis of ABC Radner project." *The Hollywood Reporter*, March 28, 2001.

Modderno, Craig. "Gene Wilder: 'I Thrive on Embarrassment!'" *Rona Barrett's Hollywood*, July 1976.

Moritz, Charles, ed. *Current Biography Yearbook 1977*. New York: The H.W. Wilson Company, 1977.

— . *Current Biography Yearbook 1978*. New York: The H.W. Wilson Company, 1978.

Nathanson, Judy, and Christine Gardener, eds. *Geneology: The Gene Wilder Fan Club Journal*, Spring 1977.

Nathanson, Judy, and Diane McDonald, eds. *Geneology: The Gene Wilder Fan Club Journal*, Fall 1979.

*New York Sunday News*, August 16, 1970.

Nicholson, Jacqui. "Gene Wilder — The 'Funny Man' Who Hides Nothing." *Rona Barrett's Hollywood*, June 1975.

Nolan, Patricia. "The Way They Were — Gene Wilder." *Rona Barrett's Hollywood*, May 1977.

O'Keefe, James. "Wilder to return to stage in Westport." *The Stamford Advocate*, May 4, 2001.

Pascua, Debbi. *Geneology: The Gene Wilder Fan Club Journal*, Fall 1978.

Piver, M. Steven, M.D., with Gene Wilder. *Gilda's Disease*. New York: Prometheus Books, 1996.

Podesta, Jane Sims. "Why Did Gilda Die?" *People*, June 3, 1991.

Pogrebin, Abigail. *Stars of David: Prominent Jews Talk About Being Jewish*. New York: Broadway Books, 2005.

Pryor, Richard. *Pryor Convictions and Other Life Sentences*. New York: Pantheon Books, 1995.

"A Quiet Battle." *People*, February 21, 2000.

Radner, Gilda. *It's Always Something*. New York: Simon and Schuster, 1989.

Richmond, Ray. *Daily Variety*, December 8, 1999.

Rosen, Diane. "Gilda!" *TV Guide*, July 29, 1978.

Rovin, Jeff. "First Films." *Video Movies*, April 1984.

Saltman, David. *Gilda: An Intimate Portrait*. Chicago: Contemporary Books, 1992.

Samuels, Jay. "Gene Wilder: Out of sadness — comedy." *Courier-Post* (Cherry Hill, NJ), January 3, 1977.

Sanello, Frank. *Eddie Murphy: The Life and Times of a Comic on the Edge.* New York: Birch Lane Press, 1997.

Schindehette, Susan. "Saturday Night Sweetheart." *People*, June 5, 1989.

Seligsohn, Leo. "On the Wilder Side." *Newsday*, December 18, 1977.

Sellers, John. "Getting Away with Murder." *TV Guide*, January 9, 1999.

Shales, Tom. "Fall TV Preview; A Dip in the Gene Pool; NBC's Refreshing 'Something Wilder'." *The Washington Post*, October 1, 1994.

Shelden, Michael. "Why would they remake Willy Wonka?" *The Daily Telegraph*, June 1, 2005.

Sinyard, Neil. *The Films of Mel Brooks.* New York: Exeter Books, 1987.

Smurthwaite, Nick, and Paul Gelder. *Mel Brooks and the Spoof Movie.* New York: Proteus Books, 1982.

Squire, Jason E., ed. *The Movie Business Book.* 2nd ed. New York: Fireside, 1992.

Steinbrunner, Chris, and Norman Michaels. *The Films of Sherlock Holmes.* New York: Citadel Press, 1978 (reissued 1991).

"Stevie Wonder Music Banned in South Africa." *The New York Times*, March 27, 1985.

Thomas, Bob. "Comeback Of Gene Wilder." *Los Angeles Herald-Examiner*, May 13, 1976.

Tynan, Kenneth. "Frolics and Detours of a Short Hebrew Man." *The New Yorker*, October 30, 1978.

Weber, Bruce. "Courtship Follies From Chekhov, Shaw and Feydeau." *The New York Times*, July 6, 2001.

Weeks, Janet. "An Awesome Alice." *TV Guide*, February 27, 1999.

"Wilder ecstatic about 'ideal wife' Carol Kane." *Valley News & Greensheet*, July 1977.

Wilder, Gene. *Kiss Me Like a Stranger: My Search for Love and Art*. New York: St. Martin's Press, 2005.

Wiley, Mason, and Damien Bona. *Inside Oscar: The Unofficial History of the Academy Awards*. New York: Ballantine Books, 1986.

Williams, John A., and Dennis A. Williams. *If I Stop I'll Die: The Comedy and Tragedy of Richard Pryor*. New York: Thunder's Mouth Press, 1991.

Wolf, Matt. "Gene Wilder makes some funny choices." Associated Press, November 6, 1996.

# Filmography

*Bonnie and Clyde* (1967)
Warner Bros.
DIRECTOR: Arthur Penn
PRODUCER: Warren Beatty
SCREENPLAY: David Newman and Robert Benton
CINEMATOGRAPHER: Burnett Guffey
EDITOR: Dede Allen
MUSIC: Charles Strouse
CAST: Warren Beatty *(Clyde Barrow)*, Faye Dunaway *(Bonnie Parker)*, Michael J. Pollard *(C.W. Moss)*, Gene Hackman *(Buck Barrow)*, Estelle Parsons *(Blanche)*, Denver Pyle *(Frank Hamer)*, Dub Taylor *(Ivan Moss)*, Evans Evans *(Velma Davis)*, Gene Wilder *(Eugene Grizzard)*
RUNNING TIME: III MINUTES

*The Producers* (1968)
Avco Embassy Pictures
DIRECTOR: Mel Brooks
PRODUCER: Sidney Glazier
SCREENPLAY: Mel Brooks
CINEMATOGRAPHER: Joseph Coffey

EDITOR: Ralph Rosenblum
MUSIC: John Morris
CAST: Zero Mostel *(Max Bialystock)*, Gene Wilder *(Leo Bloom)*, Dick Shawn *(Lorenzo St. DuBois)*, Kenneth Mars *(Franz Liebkind)*, Christopher Hewett *(Roger De Bris)*, Andreas Voutsinas *(Carmen Giya)*, Lee Meredith *(Ulla)*, Estelle Winwood *("Hold Me Touch Me")*, Renee Taylor *(Eva Braun)*, Barney Martin *(Göring)*, William Hickey *(The Drunk)*
MPAA RATING: PG
RUNNING TIME: 88 MINUTES

*Start the Revolution Without Me* (1970)
Warner Bros.
DIRECTOR: Bud Yorkin
PRODUCER: Bud Yorkin
SCREENPLAY: Fred Freeman and Lawrence J. Cohen
CINEMATOGRAPHER: Jean Tournier
EDITOR: Ferris Webster
MUSIC: John Addison
CAST: Gene Wilder *(Claude/Philippe)*, Donald Sutherland *(Charles/Pierre)*, Hugh Griffith *(King Louis)*, Jack MacGowran *(Jacques)*, Billie Whitelaw *(Queen Marie)*, Victor Spinetti *(Duke d'Escargot)*, Ewa Aulin *(Christina)*, Helen Fraser *(Mimi)*, Orson Welles *(The Narrator)*
MPAA RATING: PG
RUNNING TIME: 91 MINUTES

*Quackser Fortune Has a Cousin in the Bronx* (1970)
UMC Pictures
DIRECTOR: Waris Hussein
PRODUCERS: John H. Cushingham and Mel Howard
SCREENPLAY: Gabriel Walsh
CINEMATOGRAPHER: Gil Taylor
EDITOR: Bill Blunde
MUSIC: Michael Dress

CAST: Gene Wilder *(Quackser Fortune)*, Margot Kidder *(Zazel)*,
May Ollis *(Mrs. Fortune)*, Seamus Forde *(Mr. Fortune)*, Liz
Davis *(Kathleen Fortune)*, Caroline Tully *(Vera Fortune)*,
Eileen Colgan *(Betsy Bourke)*, David Kelly *(Maguire)*
MPAA RATING: R
RUNNING TIME: 88 MINUTES

*Willy Wonka & the Chocolate Factory* (1971)
Warner Bros.
DIRECTOR: Mel Stuart
PRODUCERS: Stan Margulies and David L. Wolper
SCREENPLAY: Roald Dahl
CINEMATOGRAPHER: Arthur Ibbetson
EDITOR: David Saxon
MUSIC: Leslie Bricusse and Anthony Newley
CAST: Gene Wilder *(Willy Wonka)*, Jack Albertson *(Grandpa
Joe)*, Peter Ostrum *(Charlie)*, Roy Kinnear *(Mr. Salt)*, Julie
Dawn Cole *(Veruca Salt)*, Leonard Stone *(Mr. Beauregarde)*,
Denise Nickerson *(Violet Beauregarde)*, Dodo Denney *(Mrs.
Teevee)*, Paris Themmen *(Mike Teevee)*, Ursula Reit *(Mrs.
Gloop)*, Michael Bollner *(Augustus Gloop)*, Diana Sowle
*(Mrs. Bucket)*, Aubrey Woods *(Bill)*, Gunter Meisner *(Mr.
Slugworth)*
MPAA RATING: G
RUNNING TIME: 98 MINUTES

*Everything You Always Wanted to Know
About Sex But Were Afraid to Ask* (1972)
United Artists
DIRECTOR: Woody Allen
PRODUCER: Charles H. Joffe
SCREENPLAY: Woody Allen
CINEMATOGRAPHER: David M. Walsh
EDITOR: Eric Albertson
MUSIC: Mundell Lowe

CAST: Woody Allen *(Victor/Fabrizio/The Fool/Sperm)*, John
     Carradine *(Doctor Bernardo)*, Lou Jacobi *(Sam)*, Louise
     Lasser *(Gina)*, Anthony Quayle *(The King)*, Tony Randall
     *(The Operator)*, Lynn Redgrave *(The Queen)*, Burt Reynolds
     *(Switchboard)*, Gene Wilder *(Doctor Ross)*, Jack Barry
     *(Himself)*, Erin Fleming *(The Girl)*, Elaine Giftos *(Mrs.
     Ross)*, Geoffrey Holder *(Sorcerer)*, Toni Holt *(Herself)*,
     Robert Q. Lewis *(Himself)*, Heather Macrae *(Helen)*,
     Pamela Mason *(Herself)*, Sidney Miller *(George)*, Regis
     Philbin *(Himself)*, Titos Vandis *(Milos)*, Robert Walden
     *(Sperm)*
MPAA RATING: R
RUNNING TIME: 87 MINUTES


*Rhinoceros* (1974)
AFT Distributing Corporation
DIRECTOR: Tom O'Horgan
PRODUCER: Ely Landau
SCREENPLAY: Julian Barry
CINEMATOGRAPHER: James Crabe
EDITOR: Bud Smith
MUSIC: Galt MacDermot
CAST: Zero Mostel *(John)*, Gene Wilder *(Stanley)*, Karen Black
     *(Daisy)*, Joe Silver *(Norman)*, Robert Weil *(Carl)*, Marilyn
     Chris *(Mrs. Bingham)*, Percy Rodrigues *(Mr. Nicholson)*,
     Robert Fields *(Young Man)*, Melody Santangelo *(Young
     Woman)*, Don Calfa *(Waiter)*, Lou Cutell *(Cashier)*,
     Howard Morton *(Doctor)*, Manuel Aviles *(Busboy)*, Anne
     Ramsey *(Lady with Cat)*, Lorna Thayer *(Restaurant Owner)*
MPAA RATING: PG
RUNNING TIME: 101 MINUTES


*Blazing Saddles* (1974)
Warner Bros.
DIRECTOR: Mel Brooks
PRODUCER: Michael Hertzberg

SCREENPLAY: Mel Brooks, Norman Steinberg, Andrew Bergman,
    Richard Pryor, Alan Uger; story by Andrew Bergman
CINEMATOGRAPHER: Joseph Biroc
EDITORS: John C. Howard and Danford Greene
MUSIC: John Morris
CAST: Cleavon Little *(Bart)*, Gene Wilder *(Jim)*, Slim Pickens
    *(Taggart)*, Mel Brooks *(Governor William J. LePetomane/*
    *Sioux Indiana Chief)*, Harvey Korman *(Hedley Lamarr)*,
    Madeline Kahn *(Lili Von Shtupp)*, David Huddleston
    *(Olsen Johnson)*, Liam Dunn *(Rev. Johnson)*, Alex Karras
    *(Mongo)*, John Hillerman *(Howard Johnson)*, George Furth
    *(Van Johnson)*, Claude Ennis Starrett, Jr. *(Gabby Johnson)*,
    Burton Gilliam *(Lyle)*, Dom DeLuise *(Buddy Bizarre)*,
    Carol Arthur *(Harriett Johnson)*
MPAA RATING: R
RUNNING TIME: 93 MINUTES

*Thursday's Game* (1974)
Made-for-TV (ABC)
DIRECTOR: Robert Moore
PRODUCER: James L. Brooks
SCREENPLAY: James L. Brooks
CINEMATOGRAPHER: Joe Biroc
EDITORS: Fredric Steinkamp and Diane Adler
MUSIC: Billy Goldenberg
CAST: Gene Wilder *(Harry Evers)*, Bob Newhart *(Marvin*
    *Ellison)*, Ellen Burstyn *(Lynn Evers)*, Cloris Leachman
    *(Lois Ellison)*, Martha Scott *(Mother)*, Nancy Walker
    *(Mrs. Bender)*, Rob Reiner *(Joel Forester)*, Valerie Harper
    *(Ann Menzente)*, Norman Fell *(Melvin Leonard)*, Gerald
    Michenaud *(David Evers)*, Richard Schaal *(Bob)*, Jed Allan
    *(Dick)*, Gino Conforti *(Mike)*, Robert Sampson *(Dave)*,
    Sidney Clute *(Camp Director)*, Chris Sarandon *(Counselor)*
RUNNING TIME: 100 MINUTES

*The Little Prince* (1974)
Paramount Pictures
DIRECTOR: Stanley Donen
PRODUCER: Stanley Donen
SCREENPLAY: Alan Jay Lerner
CINEMATOGRAPHER: Christopher Challis
EDITORS: Peter Boita and John Guthridge
MUSIC: Frederick Loewe
CAST: Richard Kiley *(The Pilot)*, Steven Warner *(The Little Prince)*,
Bob Fosse *(The Snake)*, Gene Wilder *(The Fox)*, Joss
Ackland *(The King)*, Clive Revill *(The Businessman)*, Victor
Spinetti *(The Historian)*, Graham Crowden *(The General)*,
Donna McKechnie *(The Rose)*
MPAA RATING: G
RUNNING TIME: 88 MINUTES

*Young Frankenstein* (1974)
Twentieth Century-Fox
DIRECTOR: Mel Brooks
PRODUCER: Michael Gruskoff
SCREENPLAY: Gene Wilder and Mel Brooks
CINEMATOGRAPHER: Gerald Hirschfeld
EDITOR: John C. Howard
MUSIC: John Morris
CAST: Gene Wilder *(Frederick Frankenstein)*, Peter Boyle
*(Monster)*, Marty Feldman *(Igor)*, Cloris Leachman *(Frau
Blücher)*, Teri Garr *(Inga)*, Kenneth Mars *(Inspector Kemp)*,
Madeline Kahn *(Elizabeth)*, Gene Hackman *(Blind
Hermit)*, Richard Haydn *(Herr Falkstein)*, Liam Dunn *(Mr.
Hilltop)*, Danny Goldman *(Medical Student)*
MPAA RATING: PG
RUNNING TIME: 105 MINUTES

*The Adventure of Sherlock Holmes' Smarter Brother* (1975)
Twentieth Century-Fox
DIRECTOR: Gene Wilder
PRODUCER: Richard A. Roth

SCREENPLAY: Gene Wilder
CINEMATOGRAPHER: Gerry Fisher
EDITOR: Jim Clark
MUSIC: John Morris
CAST: Gene Wilder *(Sigerson Holmes)*, Madeline Kahn *(Jenny Hill)*, Marty Feldman *(Orville Sacker)*, Dom DeLuise *(Gambetti)*, Leo McKern *(Moriarty)*, Roy Kinnear *(Moriarty's Assistant)*, John LeMuserier *(Lord Redcliff)*, Douglas Wilmer *(Sherlock Holmes)*, Thorley Walters *(Dr. Watson)*
MPAA RATING: PG
RUNNING TIME: 91 MINUTES

*Silver Streak* (1976)
Twentieth Century-Fox
DIRECTOR: Arthur Hiller
PRODUCERS: Thomas L. Miller and Edward K. Milkis
SCREENPLAY: Colin Higgins
CINEMATOGRAPHER: David M. Walsh
EDITOR: David Bretherton
MUSIC: Henry Mancini
CAST: Gene Wilder *(George Caldwell)*, Jill Clayburgh *(Hilly Burns)*, Richard Pryor *(Grover T. Muldoon)*, Patrick McGoohan *(Roger Devereau)*, Ned Beatty *(Bob Sweet)*, Clifton James *(Sheriff Chauncey)*, Ray Walston *(Mr. Whiney)*, Stefan Gierasch *(Professor Schreiner & Johnson)*, Len Birman *(Chief)*, Valerie Curtin *(Plain Jane)*, Lucille Benson *(Rita Babtree)*, Scatman Crothers *(Ralston)*, Richard Kiel *(Reace)*, Fred Willard *(Jerry Jarvis)*
MPAA RATING: PG
RUNNING TIME: 113 MINUTES

*The World's Greatest Lover* (1977)
Twentieth Century-Fox
DIRECTOR: Gene Wilder
PRODUCER: Gene Wilder
CO-PRODUCERS: Terence Marsh and Chris Greenbury

SCREENPLAY: Gene Wilder
CINEMATOGRAPHER: Gerald Hirschfeld
EDITOR: Anthony A. Pellegrino
SUPERVISING FILM EDITOR: Chris Greenbury
MUSIC: John Morris
CAST: Gene Wilder *(Rudy Valentine)*, Carol Kane *(Annie)*, Dom
    DeLuise *(Zitz)*, Fritz Feld *(Hotel Manager)*, Cousin
    Buddy *(Cousin Buddy)*, Michael Huddleston *(Barber)*,
    Carl Ballantine *(Uncle Harry)*, Ronny Graham *(Director)*,
    Danny DeVito *(Assistant Director)*, Candice Azzara
    *(Anne Calassandro)*, David Huddleston *(Boss)*, Jack Riley
    *(Projectionist)*, Sal Viscuso *(Assistant Director)*, Carol
    Arthur *(Woman in Record Store)*
MPAA RATING: PG
RUNNING TIME: 89 MINUTES

*The Frisco Kid* (1979)
Warner Bros.
DIRECTOR: Robert Aldrich
PRODUCER: Mace Neufeld
SCREENPLAY: Michael Elias and Frank Shaw
CINEMATOGRAPHER: Robert B. Hauser
EDITORS: Maury Winetrobe, Irving Rosenblum, and Jack Horger
MUSIC: Frank DeVol
CAST: Gene Wilder *(Avram Belinski)*, Harrison Ford *(Tommy
    Lillard)*, Ramon Bieri *(Mr. Jones)*, Val Bisoglio *(Chief Gray
    Cloud)*, George Ralph DiCenzo *(Darryl Diggs)*, Leo Fuchs
    *(Chief Rabbi)*, Penny Peyser *(Rosalie)*, Vincent Schiavelli
    *(Brother Bruno)*
MPAA RATING: PG
RUNNING TIME: 122 MINUTES

*Stir Crazy* (1980)
Columbia Pictures
DIRECTOR: Sidney Poitier
PRODUCER: Hannah Weinstein
SCREENPLAY: Bruce Jay Friedman

CINEMATOGRAPHER: Fred Schuler
EDITOR: Harry Keller
MUSIC: Tom Scott
CAST: Gene Wilder *(Skip Donahue)*, Richard Pryor *(Harry Monroe)*,
   Georg Stanford Brown *(Rory Schultebrand)*, JoBeth Williams
   *(Meredith)*, Miguelangel Suarez *(Jesus Ramirez)*, Craig T.
   Nelson *(Deputy Ward Wilson)*, Barry Corbin *(Warden Walter
   Beatty)*, Charles Weldon *(Blade)*, Nicolas Coster *(Warden
   Henry Sampson)*, Joel Brooks *(Len Garber)*, Jonathan Banks
   *(Jack Graham)*, Erland Van Lidth de Jeude *(Grossberger)*,
   Lewis Van Bergen *(Guard #1)*, Lee Purcell *(Susan)*, Franklin
   Ajaye *(Young Man in Hospital)*, Luis Avalos *(Chico)*
MPAA RATING: R
RUNNING TIME: III MINUTES

*Sunday Lovers* (1981)
MGM/United Artists
DIRECTORS: Bryan Forbes, Edouard Molinaro, Dino Risi, and
   Gene Wilder
PRODUCER: Leo L. Fuchs
SCREENPLAY: Age and Scarpelli, Dino Risi, Leslie Bricusse,
   Francis Veber, and Gene Wilder
CINEMATOGRAPHERS: Claude Lecomte, Claude Agostini, Tonino
   Delli Colli, and Gerald Hirschfeld
EDITORS: Philip Shaw, Robert and Monique Isnardon, Alberto
   Gallitti, and Christopher Greenbury
MUSIC: Manuel De Sica
CAST: Roger Moore *(Harry)*, Ugo Tognazzi *(Armando)*, Lino
   Ventura *(François Quérole)*, Gene Wilder *(Skippy)*,
   Kathleen Quinlan *(Laurie)*, Lynn Redgrave *(Lady Davina)*,
   Denholm Elliott *(Parker)*, Priscilla Barnes *(Donna)*,
   Sylva Koscina *(Zaira)*, Beba Loncar *(Marisa)*, Rossana
   Podesta *(Clara)*, Catherine Salviat *(Christine)*, Milena
   Vukotic *(Nora)*, Robert Webber *(Henry Morrison)*, Dianne
   Crittenden *(Psychiatrist)*, Luis Avalos *(Roommate)*
MPAA RATING: R
RUNNING TIME: I27 MINUTES

*Hanky Panky* (1982)
Columbia Pictures
DIRECTOR: Sidney Poitier
PRODUCER: Martin Ransohoff
SCREENPLAY: Henry Rosenbaum and David Taylor
CINEMATOGRAPHER: Arthur Ornitz
EDITOR: Harry Keller
MUSIC: Tom Scott
CAST: Gene Wilder *(Michael Jordon)*, Gilda Radner *(Kate
    Hellman)*, Kathleen Quinlan *(Janet Dunn)*, Richard
    Widmark *(Ransom)*, Robert Prosky *(Hiram Calder)*, Josef
    Sommer *(Adrian Pruitt)*, Johnny Sekka *(Lacey)*, Jay
    O. Sanders *(Katz)*, Sam Gray *(Dr. John Wolff)*, Larry
    Bryggman *(Stacy)*, Pat Corley *(Pilot)*, Johnny Brown *(Bus
    Driver)*, Doris Belack *(Building Manager)*
MPAA RATING: PG
RUNNING TIME: 110 MINUTES

*The Woman in Red* (1984)
Orion Pictures
DIRECTOR: Gene Wilder
PRODUCER: Victor Drai
SCREENPLAY: Gene Wilder
CINEMATOGRAPHER: Fred Schuler
EDITOR: Christopher Greenbury
MUSIC: John Morris
CAST: Gene Wilder *(Theodore Pierce)*, Charles Grodin *(Buddy)*,
    Joseph Bologna *(Joe)*, Judith Ivey *(Didi)*, Michael
    Huddleston *(Michael)*, Kelly LeBrock *(Charlotte)*, Gilda
    Radner *(Ms. Milner)* , Kyle T. Heffner *(Richard)*, Michael
    Zorek *(Shelly)*
MPAA RATING: PG-13
RUNNING TIME: 87 MINUTES

*Haunted Honeymoon* (1986)
Orion Pictures
DIRECTOR: Gene Wilder

PRODUCER: Susan Ruskin
SCREENPLAY: Gene Wilder and Terence Marsh
CINEMATOGRAPHER: Fred Schuler
EDITOR: Chris Greenbury
MUSIC: John Morris
CAST: Gene Wilder *(Larry Abbot)*, Gilda Radner *(Vickie Pearle)*,
    Dom DeLuise *(Aunt Kate)*, Jonathan Pryce *(Charles)*, Paul
    L. Smith *(Paul Abbot)*, Peter Vaughan *(Francis Abbot Sr.)*,
    Bryan Pringle *(Pfister)*, Jim Carter *(Montego)*, Eve Ferret
    *(Sylvia)*, Roger Ashton-Griffiths *(Francis Jr.)*, Jo Ross
    *(Susan)*, Ann Way *(Rachel)*, Julann Griffin *(Nora)*
MPAA RATING: PG
RUNNING TIME: 82 MINUTES

*See No Evil, Hear No Evil* (1989)
Tri-Star Pictures
DIRECTOR: Arthur Hiller
PRODUCER: Marvin Worth
SCREENPLAY: Earl Barret, Arne Sultan, Eliot Wald, Andrew
    Kurtzman, and Gene Wilder; story by Earl Barret, Arne
    Sultan, and Marvin Worth
CINEMATOGRAPHER: Victor J. Kemper
EDITOR: Robert C. Jones
MUSIC: Stewart Copeland
CAST: Richard Pryor *(Wally)*, Gene Wilder *(Dave)*, Joan
    Severance *(Eve)*, Kevin Spacey *(Kirgo)*, Alan North
    *(Braddock)*, Anthony Zerbe *(Sutherland)*, Louis Giambalvo
    *(Gatlin)*, Kirsten Childs *(Adele)*
MPAA RATING: R
RUNNING TIME: 103 MINUTES

*Funny About Love* (1990)
Paramount Pictures
DIRECTOR: Leonard Nimoy
PRODUCERS: Jon Avnet and Jordan Kerner
SCREENPLAY: Norman Steinberg and David Frankel
CINEMATOGRAPHER: Fred Murphy

EDITOR: Peter E. Berger
MUSIC: Miles Goodman
CAST: Gene Wilder *(Duffy Bergman)*, Christine Lahti *(Meg)*, Mary Stuart Masterson *(Daphne)*, Robert Prosky *(E.T.)*, Stephen Tobolowsky *(Hugo)*, Anne Jackson *(Adele)*, Susan Ruttan *(Claire)*, Jean DeBaer *(Vivian)*, David Margulies *(Dr. Benjamin)*, Regis Philbin *(Himself)*, Patrick Ewing *(Himself)*
MPAA RATING: PG-13
RUNNING TIME: 101 MINUTES

*Another You* (1991)
Tri-Star Pictures
DIRECTOR: Maurice Phillips
PRODUCER: Ziggy Steinberg
SCREENPLAY: Ziggy Steinberg
CINEMATOGRAPHER: Victor J. Kemper
EDITOR: Dennis M. Hill
MUSIC: Charles Gross
CAST: Richard Pryor *(Eddie Dash)*, Gene Wilder *(George/ Abe Fielding)*, Mercedes Ruehl *(Elaine)*, Stephen Lang *(Dibbs)*, Vanessa Williams *(Gloria)*, Phil Rubenstein *(Al)*, Peter Michael Goetz *(Therapist)*, Billy Beck *(Harry)*, Jerry Houser *(Tim)*, Kevin Pollak *(Phil)*, Craig Richard Nelson *(Walt)*, Kandis Chappell *(Gail)*, Vincent Schiavelli *(Dentist)*
MPAA RATING: R
RUNNING TIME: 98 MINUTES

*Murder in a Small Town* (1999)
Made-for-TV (A&E)
DIRECTOR: Joyce Chopra
PRODUCERS: Fred Berner and Steven Paul
SCREENPLAY: Gilbert Pearlman and Gene Wilder
CINEMATOGRAPHER: Bruce Surtees
EDITOR: Peter C. Frank

MUSIC: John Morris
CAST: Gene Wilder *(Cash Carter)*, Mike Starr *(Tony)*, Cherry
    Jones *(Mimi)*, Frances Conroy *(Martha Lassiter)*, Deidre
    O'Connell *(Kate Faxton)*, Terry O'Quinn *(Sidney Lassiter)*,
    Ebon Moss-Bachrach *(Billy)*, Elizabeth Rosen *(Sophie
    Carter)*, Matthew Edison *(Albert Lassiter)*, Carlo Rota
    *(Charles)*
RUNNING TIME: 100 MINUTES

*Alice in Wonderland* (1999)
Made-for-TV (NBC)
DIRECTOR: Nick Willing
PRODUCER: Dyson Lovell
SCREENPLAY: Peter Barnes
CINEMATOGRAPHER: Giles Nuttgens
EDITOR: Alex Mackie
MUSIC: Richard Hartley
CAST: Tina Majorino *(Alice)*, Robbie Coltrane *(Ned Tweedledum)*,
    Whoopi Goldberg *(Cheshire Cat)*, Ben Kingsley *(Major
    Caterpillar)*, Christopher Lloyd *(White Knight)*, Pete
    Postlethwaite *(Carpenter)*, Miranda Richardson *(Queen
    of Hearts)*, Martin Short *(Mad Hatter)*, Peter Ustinov
    *(Walrus)*, George Wendt *(Fred Tweedledee)*, Gene Wilder
    *(Mock Turtle)*
RUNNING TIME: 130 MINUTES

*The Lady in Question* (1999)
Made-for-TV (A&E)
DIRECTOR: Joyce Chopra
PRODUCERS: Stan Margulies, Craig McNeil, and Steven Paul
SCREENPLAY: Gene Wilder and Gilbert Pearlman
CINEMATOGRAPHER: Bruce Surtees
EDITOR: Angelo Corrao
MUSIC: John Morris
CAST: Gene Wilder *(Cash Carter)*, Mike Starr *(Tony Rossini)*,
    Cherry Jones *(Mimi Barnes)*, Barbara Sukowa *(Rachel
    Singer)*, John Benjamin Hickey *(Paul Kessler)*, Michael

Cumpsty *(Gruber/Wheeler)*, Claire Bloom *(Emma Sachs)*, Daniel Serafini-Sauli *(Rudy Bernheim)*, Kerry McPherson *(Dorie Bernheim)*, Dixie Seatle *(Gertie Moser)*, Kate Trotter *(Lady with Veil)*

RUNNING TIME: 94 MINUTES

# Index

# About the Author

BRIAN SCOTT MEDNICK is a graduate of NYU film school. He is an author, critic, and filmmaker whose writing has appeared in many magazines and newspapers. He lives in New York City.

www.brianscottmednick.com

BOB DAVIS

CPSIA information can be obtained at www.ICGtesting.com
Printed in the USA
BVOW041629241012

303800BV00005B/309/P

9 781593 936211